P
91
.M28

McLuhan
     Verbi-voco-visual
explorations

About the Cover:

The basic design of the cover derives from the spherical nature of the oral world. Verbi-Voco-Visual standing for the word as sound ($\pi\epsilon\iota\rho\omega$) and as sight (hieroglyphs). The hieroglyphs are placed on a curve, the lower curve, reading from left to right means "looking for the ways" and the top curve reading from right to left means "speech".

EXPLORING THE WORD!

VERBI-
VOCO-
VISUAL
EXPLORATIONS

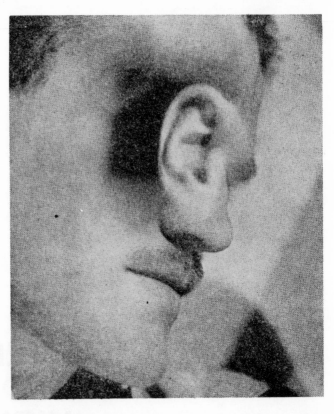

From VISION IN MOTION by L. Moholy-Nagy, 1947. Permission by Paul Theobald and Company, Publishers, Chicago 60602.

/VERBI-VOCO-VISUAL EXPLORATIONS)

by Marshall McLuhan

with additional contributions by V. J. Papanek
J. B. Bessinger
Marshall McLuhan
Karl Polanyi
Carol C. Hollis
David Hogg
Jack Jones

1967
Something Else Press, Inc.
New York   Frankfurt   Villefranche-sur-Mer

CONTENTS

Acknowledgments

This book was originally issued as Number 8 of EXPLORATIONS, a periodical edited by Marshall McLuhan and Edmund Carpenter, and published by the University of Toronto under the sponsorship of the Telegram of Toronto and through a grant from the Ford Foundation. We have re-issued it with some revisions and with some changes in the original design which was done by Mr. Harley Parker of the Royal Ontario Museum in Toronto.

In addition Something Else Press, Inc. wishes to thank the authors of the various articles reprinted here for their cooperation, and also to thank authors, copyright holders and publishers for allowing excerpts from the following works to be quoted:

HOW THE SOVIET SYSTEM WORKS, by Raymond A. Bauer, Alex Inkeles and Clyde Kluckohn. Harvard University Press 1956.
LITURGICAL PIETY, by Father Louis Bouyer. University of Notre Dame Press, Notre Dame–London 1955.
THE TURN OF THE TIDE by Sir Arthur Bryant. Copyright © 1957 by Arthur Bryant. Reprinted by permission of William Collins Sons and Co., Ltd., London and Glasgow, and Doubleday & Company, Inc., New York.
PERSONAL REVOLUTION AND PICASSO by Louis Danz. Originally published by Longmans, Green & Company 1941. Reprinted by permission of David McKay Company, Inc., New York.
THE WAY BEYOND ART by Alexander Dorner. New York University Press 1958.
THE USE OF POETRY AND THE USE OF CRITICISM and SELECTED ESSAYS by T. S. Eliot. Faber and Faber Ltd., London, and Harvard University Press.
THE PSYCHOANALYTICAL THEORY OF NEUROSIS by Otto Fenichel. W. W. Norton & Company, New York 1945, and The Cresset Press, Ltd., London.
THE PEOPLE OF GREAT RUSSIA by Geoffrey Gorer and John Rickman. W. W. Norton & Company, New York 1962, and The Cresset Press, Ltd., London.

VERBI-
VOCO-
VISUAL
EXPLORATIONS

BRAIN STORMING

The Strange Case of Minerva's  HOWL

1 Minerva, Goddess of Ideas, sprang fully armed from the head of Zeus. Ideas and suggestions belong entirely to the oral side of our culture, which is becoming more important daily. The business world finds this very confusing. Business still works by chain of written command.

In the *New Yorker* of April 13, 1957, there was printed a correspondence between poet Marianne Moore and an official of the Ford Motor Company. The official explained that there was facing the company a problem, which was more in the field of words and the evanescent meaning of words than in car-making. His dilemma was a name for a rather important new series of cars.

Miss Moore as poet, always deals with oral problems. The problem of the Ford Motor Company was an oral problem. An auditory problem in the public dimensions of words. The deal simply could not proceed since a bureaucratic business structure has to process all problems by written channels. The official insisted that the procedures of the business world required that the Company inscribe a formal agreement with provision for a suitable fee before proceeding in the matter.

"Peebles, we've found the proposals you've been dropping into the suggestion box not only stimulating but provocative—so much so, in fact, that we'd feel guilty confining a man of your alertness and ingenuity within the limits of your present position. Effective the first of the month, therefore, we're releasing you from our employ."

Drawing by CEM, copr. © 1950, The New Yorker Magazine, Inc.

It is this being locked into the patterns of explicit typography which compels business to hire all idea aid on a pre-arranged salary or consultant fee basis. An idea may be worth millions to a business but it can only be paid for as a written package. And the fees are thus peanuts, having no relation to the total and inclusive nature of ideas. Neither the idea people nor the business bureaucracies understand the peculiar oral-written clash which frustrates them. The case of Marianne Moore and the Ford Motor Company is a classic of cultural conflict and misunderstanding which is heading for much more dramatic developments in our electronic era.

A 1953 book by Charles E. Redfield, *Communication in Management,* reads like an eighteenth-century book of military strategy in comparison with the realities with which it pretends to grapple. Yet the strategy of this book is quite as realistic as the executive world. That is to say, scarcely aware of anything.

Only very slowly and gradually is the business head getting penetrated by the fact that instantaneous information flow and instantaneous electronic processing of complex data mean the end of the old bureaucratic ways and procedures.

From the viewpoint of any established procedure, any new fact or idea whatever is a menace. Since all government and business establishments in our day are still based on written processing they naturally view all oral development as disruptive.

Until inventors got their work put on a written basis in the nineteenth century they were robbed 100 per cent. Thereafter they were robbed only 99.9 per cent. The idea man is in the same position today. He can be paid only as offering services inside the written procedures of the business concerned.

The greatest inventions, the most valuable ideas can always be stated in a few words. The reason for this is basic. An idea is an oral thing because it is based on instant awareness of a total situation. Oral means "total" primarily, "spoken" accidentally.

American research labs and business spend billions on research yet notoriously produce no ideas or inventions at all. They do not permit themselves the oral totality of approach necessary to "intuition". Instead, they take ideas from solitary persons who exist outside all organizations, and they give lineal, written processing or application to these. Technology is explicitness. Invention or creation is implicitness. Technology is written explication. Intuition and invention are oral, total, implicit, inclusive, simultaneous.

But electronics no longer permit the patient, plodding, systematic man to go his sluggish mental ways. Electronics mean that even business and bureaucracy must become oral and inventive. Hence the brainstorming session. It is the anguished effort of the bureaucrat to keep the new oral demands of electronic simultaneity in the groove of lineality.

Instead of the inward gaze of Minerva's owl there rises from the collective couch of bureaucratic inquisition a discordant howl.

There needs must be this evil of brains in India, but woe to him through whom they are increased! The feeling grew that Mr. Fielding was a disruptive force, and rightly, for ideas are fatal to caste, and he used ideas by that most potent method—interchange.

E. M. Forster, *A Passage to India*

The American looks in the dictionary for the meaning of the word. The Englishman looks to find out what's wrong with the definition provided by the dictionary. To a degree far beyond any other area of the English-speaking world the U.S.A. is literary in the sense of having been shaped by the printing press

2 Its technology is an extension of the Gutenberg assembly lines. Its habits of mind have been formed more by the printed word than those of England, because the main form of culture and communication which came to America was print. The other forms were not transportable so readily or cheaply. Here is William Cobbett contrasting the Americans and the English in 1795.

There are very few really *ignorant* men in America of native growth. Every farmer is more or less of a *reader*. There is no *brogue*, no *provincial dialect*. No class like that which the French call *peasantry* . . . . they are all well-informed; modest without shyness; always free to communicate what they know, and never ashamed to acknowledge they have yet to learn. You never hear them *boast* of their possessions, and you never hear them *complaining* of their wants. They have all been readers from their youth up; and there are few subjects on which they cannot converse with you whether of a political or a scientific nature. At any rate they always *hear* with patience. I do not know that I ever heard a native American interrupt another man while he was speaking. Their *sedateness* and *coolness*, the *deliberate* manner in which they say and do everything, and the *slowness* and *reserve* with which they express their assent; these are very wrongly estimated when they are taken for marks of a *want of feeling*. It must be a tale of woe indeed, that will bring a tear from an American's eye; but any trumped-up story will send his hand to his pocket... However, you will not, for a long while, know what to do for want of the *quick responses* of the English tongue, and the decided tone of the English expression. The *loud voice* and the *hard squeeze* by the hand; the *instant assent* or *dissent*; the clamorous joy, *the bitter wailing*; the ardent friendship; the deadly enmity; the love that makes people kill themselves; the hatred that makes them kill others. All these belong to the characters of Englishmen, in whose minds and hearts every feeling exists in the *extreme*.

Cobbett here provides a list of opposing characteristics that belong to written and oral cultures. Since his day Englishmen have undergone the same treatment of print culture *via* compulsory education as made the very prim and sedate American of 1795 a phenomenon to Cobbett. Likewise the heavy influx of noisy emotional influences from the oral cultures of Ireland and middle Europe have obliterated some of the American characteristics of 1795 except among school teachers and the professoriat. In the same way the oral character of the American South has swamped the North since talkies, radio and LP have given it precedence over the print culture of the North.

WHAT ABOUT THOSE GRIM LINEAL GROMYKOS?

The whole Russian effort has been slanted to produce the very type of Cobbett's American (Model 1795). The Russian wants to get rid of the Englishman (Model 1795) because that oral type he has produced by the 100 million for centuries.

The American model 1795 is the inner-directed man whose life runs on the hard rails of typography and self-improvement. It was an exciting cultural novelty to discover how to turn out this type of man and then to watch him steam off along the entrepreneurial rails towards distant and prestigious stations.

The intense individualism and even more ferocious nationalism that is born out of the same print-processing is just now being discovered in the Soviet area. It will eventually splinter the Soviet area as effectively as it splintered England and Europe in the sixteenth century.

Is it not strange that the Marxists should have no awareness of the means of communication as the constitutive social factor? That Marx should not have noticed that English and American industry were merely projections of print technology?

WHY DID MARX MISS THE COMMUNICATION BUS?

For many centuries the Soviet area has been as oral as a pre-literate society. The Greek Orthodox Church has an oral tradition compared to the legalistic and individual Roman tradition.

As Geoffrey Gorer puts it in *The People of Great Russia*:
The central sacrament of Western Christianity is *Communion*, the intimate connexion between the individual worshipper and Jesus Christ; in the Orthodox Church the central experience is *Sobornost*, the Pentecostal descent of the Holy Ghost on the whole congregation simultaneously.

Now launched on a program entirely antithetic to their oral culture the Russians naturally ignore and discount all that is basic in their own make-up. We would be idiots to do likewise.

IDIOT {
Greek for a
private person
most mysterious
entity to a
Russian of any
century
}

ELECTRONICS AS E.S.P.

3 When a pilot has no visual or auditory direction he "flies by the seat of his pants".
When a business man is lost in the bush or is confronted with such complexity that he can find no plausible line to follow, he "plays it by ear". When a business man is baffled by a situation he asks to have it "spelled out". He likes to have a fine "line of goods". He likes his salesmen to "talk a good line". When a man talks a good line he is flattered when told that "it listens good".

Our world is rapidly hastening from the monolithic fixity of the man who says "from where I'm sitting" to the multiple-layered vision of the jet pilot. Are we changing from

BIRD WATCHERS TO

Code for the *Hidden Persuaders

Until musical scores were printed there was no other way of organizing musical work except by song mode. With printed scores instrumentation could supplant voice. Today the return to vocal modes even in instrumental music is typical of the Western insistence on oral complexity. In a symphony orchestra the players are as little able to hear the music as the hands on an assembly line to see the whole.

SYNESTHESIA the new sin of the nineteenth century roused as much misunderstanding as E.S.P. today. Extra sensory perception is normal perception. Today electronics are extra sensory, Gallup polls and motivation research are also. Therefore people get all steamed up about E.S.P. as something for the future. It is already past and present.

Synesthesia is simply totalism in the use of the senses. After centuries of abstract, printed lineality the Baudelaires and Rimbauds revolted into synesthesia because the telegraphic and photographic resources of the earlier nineteenth century had suddenly revealed the possibility of simultaneous experience at many levels. Wagner leapt at the possibilities. The *Bauhaus* gave institutional form to the same developments. Today we take the entire *Bauhaus* program of Synesthesia for granted as normal suburban living. The tactile sculpture, the bleached stump, as much as the bleached blonde, have supplanted the conch shell, the aspidistra and the peignoir as properties of the suburban scene.

The most ordinary ads feature all the Cubist and Dada gimmicks "as dumb as old medallions to the thumb" which put us inside and outside every situation simultaneously.

Imagine people in 1910 being baffled by visual cubism when they wallowed in it in their newspapers every day! The difficulty is not to explain cubism but to account for the mental processes of those who found it obscure.

Color systems today are still lineal because of industrial bias: "the Munsell color sphere is not a sphere at all but a series of psychologically graduated lines". We have to get inside the color sphere to control it! It's like a jet plane. The Parker color sphere makes the observer the sphere. Pilot and plane are one.

Sculpture has discovered the auditory world. Sculptors know that the cello and musical instruments are perfect relations of auditory space.

Keyboard instruments are closely related to print technology. Carl Orff, the composer, has a school in Vienna for training in musical appreciation. He argues that by the time a child can read and write it is already too late to train the ear. The keyboard kills all musical sense.

We are rapidly re-creating

on an enormous global scale

the pre-industrial world of

THE BE-SPOKE TAILOR

4 In England there are still tailors whose know-how is not available for a price. NOT until a worthy and prestigious figure from the proper class has be-spoken you, can you command the tailor's services. This situation was normal in the pre-industrial world of crafts. It still obtains among portrait painters to some degree.

Today, however, the know-how of industry itself is only available when the public has spoken through the numerous channels of motivation research. When market analysis reassures the industrialist that the public has given its imprimatur then he produces. Anything that has to be produced can be invented later.

The older industrial procedure was the same as older literary procedure. You made something or said something and then went in search of a market or an audience. So that literary minds were scandalized when Mr. Eliot said that "the only way of expressing emotion in the form of art is by finding an objective correlative; in other words, a set of objects, a situation, a chain of events which shall be the formula of that *particular* emotion; . . ." That is to say work backwards from effect to cause. Establish the effect before you even know what will be the cause of that effect.

This is the way detective stories are written, and the way all modern production is achieved. The method of trial and error is too costly and wasteful (as well as too imprecise) to be tolerated in a global society.

We have to know what we are doing in advance.

We have to repeat what we were about to say.

"The acoustics of Dublin are perfect," said George Moore.

"The acoustics of the Maple Leaf Stadium are poor," says Rocket Richard, the French-Canadian hockey player whose puck rides on the roar of the crowd.

History as she is harped. Rite words by Rote order. Listening to the simultaneous messages of Dublin, Joyce released the greatest flood of oral linguistic music that was ever manipulated into art.

THE JOURNALIST'S DILEMMA

OR

The Fox and His Gripes

5 Unlike the business world the world of the newspaper is mainly oral in pattern. The anguish of the newsmen is the reverse of that of the neurosis of business men. The business man today is trying to twist his habitual lineality into the likeness of an oral sphere. For a century the men of the press have been torn by the wish to look or sound like men of letters.

The simultaneous aspect of the newspaper page reveals at once its oral character: many stories, many scenes at a glance. Nowadays the headline (which has always been admitted to scream loudly) has been given the further oral task of compression. An entire story has to go into it, as the whole of a novel into its title.

The press could not avoid assuming an oral form from the time that it came to rely on the telegraph. The instantaneous flow of information put the oral pattern on every phase of the press thereafter. Hence the choice of press form by the Art Manifesto.

The newspaper-office world is a buzzing oral world bursting with ideas and human interest gossip. It is the world of the collective *entre nous* and *sub rosa* confidences.

Antithetic to the newspaper-office world is the solitary study of the silent literary man. The literary page is the slowly processed single perspective world, loaded with the prestige and asceticism which evoke the sentimental longing of the newsman.

In America, however, literature itself is almost entirely the product of journalists. The newspaper has transformed the character of letters. Whitman, Poe, Twain, and, in our time, Stephen Crane, Hemingway, and nearly all of our other writers have been men of the daily press.

But the split between the two worlds has grown wider in the hearts of the press men themselves. It is the perennial theme of their nostalgic reveries and conversation.

ORAL MAN idolizes the literary

LITERARY MAN dreams of oral conquests

Ezra Pound says "Poetry is news that stays news." He invaded the oral sphere and became news—an arduous metamorphosis.

**The most obvious feature of any oral situation is
extreme flexibility in immediate foreground and
extreme persistence or rigidity in over-all pattern**

6 André Malraux is as apt an instance of the oral or auditory man as Churchill. Picked up at the roadside one day by his friend Sylvia Beach who had not seen him for seven years he began: "Anyway, the whole point about Etruscan . . ."
It was only later that she recalled that they had been discussing this matter when interrupted seven years before.

An oral society like the Arabs seems very flighty, amorphous and shifting to casual observers. Compared to England or America it is monolithic in its consistency and permanence.

England is an oral world only in comparison with USA. Compared with France or Latin countries England represents a high degree of conditioning by print technology. English policy has always seemed utterly inconsistent and wavering to the French. Yet the English present an immediate *façade* of great stability. England has undergone far more change and revolution than the "excitable" "unstable" and oral French nation. Simone de Beauvoir in *The Mandarins* speaks of the French language today as a P.A. system that has gone dead. Only an oral people would dream of regarding their language as a public address system. English is now a world P.A. system but we would never think to say so. English is more of a mass medium than radio.

A people whose officials are entirely products of written procedure are quite indifferent to long-term rigidity or consistency, because, while, the page in itself is rigid its effect is psychic ferment.

Only oral peoples have any memory for the past, which, for them, is always present. A literary people entrusts its memory to its scribes not its bards. For the Irish as for the American South the past is now. To a literary society this habit of mind appears fantastic and morbid.

IT SEEMS HISTORY IS TO BLAME

Haines the Englishman in *Ulysses* sympathizes with Stephen for the wrongs done to Ireland:

> I can quite understand that, he said calmly. An Irishman must think like that, I daresay. We feel in England that we have treated you rather unfairly. It seems history is to blame.

For Stephen of the Irish oral tradition on the other hand, "History is a nightmare from which I am trying to awake." In *Finnegans Wake* the entire life and experience of the race is compressed in simultaneous present in true bardic style.

HOW THE SOVIET SYSTEM WORKS — In *How the Soviet System Works* Raymond A. Bauer, Alex Inkeles, and Clyde Kluckohn report at length on the long-term rigidity of the Soviet strategy:

> To turn to the other pole: tactical flexibility . . . the leadership is characterized by extreme flexibility in many of its short-run goals in a way that has been much noted and marvelled at in the West.

Our incapacity to envisage or sustain any long-term projects, while putting on an impressive front of sober determination, must raise similar wonder in the Soviet.

How the Soviet System Works is an elaborate documentation of an oral culture. To an oral people the acceptance of monarchic structure alone makes sense. Our own technology increasingly imposes the same structure on business and industry. For an oral people it is the age-old habit of simultaneity and inclusiveness which demands orientation in and towards a single consciousness. For ourselves it is this same character emerging unsought and misunderstood from our electronic media which beckons towards the same condition.

Our electronic media now create focal points of information which are monopolies resisted in vain by the press. In striking contrast is the situation of George Washington who had been in office less than six weeks when he had to invoke the reporting clause of the constitution to get from his cabinet officers "a general idea of the affairs of the United States". Until these written reports were available the head executive did not know what was going on.

By contrast the Soviet headache is what they call "Familyness". Their problem is to avoid the natural face-to-face loyalties by encouraging criticism of bureaucrats and concentrating all concern on the leadership. A notable feature of all oral organization appears again and again in *How the Soviet System Works*:

RUSSIAN STORM AND AMERICAN CRASH

"The characteristic Soviet approach to problems is that of "storming", i.e., tackling (on the domestic scene) one or a limited number of objectives at a time and hitting them hard, largely ignoring side effects." (p.51)

With us the *crash* program is a natural development of our technology. With the Russian as with the Celt it is temperament-preference. It appears in their military operations naturally. Theirs is an "armed horde" guided by the spoken word, plus a small *élite* corps of modern bureaucratic type. This small corps is extremely efficient, mobile, aware. The rest of the army dispenses with all that we consider normal to such organization. It relies on its own improvisation for most of its food and transport. Fitzroy MacLean gives an idea of it in *Eastern Approaches*:

Twenty miles or so south of Belgrade we emerged on to the main road and joined a continuous stream of Red Army trucks, tanks and guns flowing northwards into battle. One thing in particular struck us now, as it had struck us from the first, namely, that every Soviet truck we saw contained one of two things: petrol or ammunition. Of rations, blankets, spare boots or clothing there was no trace. The presumption was that such articles, if they were required at all, were provided at the expense of the enemy or of the local population. Almost every man we saw was a fighting soldier. What they carried with them were materials of war in the narrowest sense. We were witnessing a return to the administrative methods of Attila and Genghis Khan, and the results seemed to deserve careful attention. For there could be no doubt that here lay one reason for the amazing speed of the Red Army's advance across Europe. Thinking it over, and recalling the number of dentists' chairs and filing cabinets which were said to have been landed in Normandy at an early stage of the Allied invasion,

I wondered whether we ourselves could not perhaps profit to some extent by the Russian example.

In regard to education the Soviet with might and main strives to obliterate every traditional feature of the oral character. But being mainly unaware of the psycho-dynamics of print technology, as they are unaware of the implications of their own oral character, they blunder about with the same monolithic writhings and gropings as we do in an opposite direction.

While our *élites* sentimentalize over pre-literate characteristics the Soviet is frantic to acquire the stolid Puritanic countenance and the Prussian procedures of the man of newly-acquired literacy.

Geoffrey Gorer tells of the pre-revolution schools for the upper castes in Russia with their dance, drama and elocution lessons in the expression of the emotions. These activities were eagerly pursued by the peasants too during their long winters:
> "The Soviet *élites* have been most deeply opposed to this proclivity of the mass of the Russians, and have done everything possible by education and edict to force its abandonment." (p.150)

The suppression of emotion is the first requisite of the new bureaucrat. Here is a directive to school-teachers in 1946 provided by Geoffrey Gorer. It displays the same sentimental idealization of the, to us, banal patterns which appear to them so difficult of attainment:
> Moral demands must always be made upon school-children in a decisive form and carried into life with firm insistence . . . Consistency must be observed by all adults who share in the rearing of the young. The several teachers of a given child should not contradict each other, but rather should follow a single line.

The lineality which patterns even our unconscious living after centuries of literacy seems so exotically desirable to a Russian as to provide the basic metaphor for "the party line".

The Puritanical firmness and consistency so hard to attain for the Russian is as much oohed and aahed over by them as a sense of humor is idealized in highly literate society.

7 Decades ago Lewis Mumford noted the American bathroom as the last sanctuary of privacy. He spoke of sight not sound. The acoustics of the tile bathroom made an ideal audition chamber for the grievances and the mimetic compensations of the North American male. Aided by shaving mirror, the acoustics of the American bathroom are perfectly suited to the inflation and rehabilitation of down-trodden males.

THE BATHROOM BARITONE AND THE WIDE OPEN SPACES

The "bathroom baritone" is as much a part of our urban folk-lore as the "strong silent man of the wide-open spaces". Having no bathroom the man from open space has no alternative but silence. And having no acoustic chamber in which to try out many moods and faces and roles he lives an empty dead-pan life. So when he does give voice it is with a sickening moan of self-pity without variety or imagination.

Oral cultures and temperaments are mobile and transitory in their moods. They glorify stability and stolidity as utopian. The mock dead-pan of the Ed Sullivans or of Irish wits is exactly like the Russian idealizing of the Puritanical imperturbability of the Gromykos or the new bureaucrats. These poses are so far from the actualities of their emotional experience as to seem superb achievements.

Corresponding to the acoustics of the American bathroom was the medieval carrell or reading booth. Here the scribe or student could play the gamut of tones as he read his manuscript (silent reading was unknown and impracticable before print). Today the Hi-fi or telephone booth are other evidences of the return to oral culture. In the novels of John Wain and Kingsley Amis, the literate English have been shocked at characters who freely express a variety of *idiotic* attitudes and poses as cathartic expedients. The white man's burden they repudiate. They toss off the constraints of typographic lineality in favour of a many-levelled oral and dramatic life.

In the Elizabethan period the English were by-words in Europe as unstable imitators of any novelty. That was the hey-day of English oral culture. Oral peoples are whimsical and arbitrary in immediate behaviour, rigid and consistent in the long run.

The oral man is a brain-picker and a brain-stormer. The organization man, Mr. Whyte assures us, would be ashamed to be caught reading during business hours. Any activity so private, silent and meditative is disloyal to the ways of organization.

THE NEW ORGANIZATION MAN IS AN ORAL MAN WITH A HEART OF TYPE

STRESS

8 Dr. Hans Selye has come up with the first non-visual disease theory since the Greeks introduced the image of the skin as an envelope enclosing organs. His *stress* theory is entirely a *field* view of disease. The body is part of a total field.

The Greek view of the body as package of organs and humors got cut down, at the Renaissance, to a view of the body as a pumping station. Then with the rise of chemistry in the nineteenth century the body became a chemistry factory. Everybody was loaded with germs. But the rise of field theory in physics now has its medical counterpart in Dr. Hans Selye's stress view. He rejects the idea that each disease has a specific cause which must be found and isolated in order for cure to occur. In a word he regards as unreal and out-dated the lineal view of disease as specific target for which a specific *shot* is indicated.

Dr. Selye wrote in *Explorations* no. 1 that:
experimental work in animals (1936) demonstrated that the organism responds in a stereotyped manner to a variety of factors such as infections, intoxications, trauma, nervous strain, heat, cold, muscular fatigue or X-irradiation . . . Their only common feature was that they placed the body in a state of general (systemic) stress. We therefore concluded that this stereotyped response, which was superimposed

upon the specific effects, represented the somatic manifestations of non-specific stress itself.

The field theory finds unnecessary the cell theory of Schleiden and Schwann (1839), just as in physics it detaches itself from the visual closed system of Newtonian mechanics.

The Selye theory becomes at once intelligible and acceptable in our twentieth century of oral awareness. That "all vital phenomena depend merely upon quantitative variations in the activation of pre-existent elementary targets" is not a superficial view in terms of auditory space.

In the old lineal terms, quantitative relations mean the exclusion of most meaning and of all spiritual complexity. A mere sequence of such effects can contain no vital or analogical drama of proportions. But analogy is itself field theory or vision such as disappeared from philosophy in the sixteenth century.

The analogical drama of being and perception needs no more than the quantitative terms postulated by Selye. With these the living word constitutes and manifests itself in all mental and spiritual complexity.

Analogical proportion is a basic aspect of auditory space and of oral culture. It is the oral equivalent of the golden section in architecture and design.

ORAL—anal

9 Otto Fenichel in *The Psychoanalytic Theory of Neuroses* describes the oral concept of Freud as follows:

> All positive or negative emphasis on taking and receiving indicates an oral origin. Unusually pronounced oral satisfaction results in a remarkable self-assurance and optimism. . . . Exceptional oral deprivation, on the other hand, determines a pessimistic (depressive) or sadistic (redress-demanding) attitude. If a person remains fixated to the world of oral wishes, he will, in his general behaviour, present a disinclination to take care of himself . . . Thus both marked generosity and marked niggardliness may be attributed to conflicts around oral eroticism. (N.Y. 1945, pp. 488–90)

Fenichel describes the correlative anal character as frugal, orderly, obstinate, likely to be concerned with saving money and with time schedules. Greedy and fond of collecting things for the sake of collecting.

In a culture which for centuries has been as lineally arranged as our own, it is obvious that the habits called "anal" or "oral" by psychologists receive a collective educational stress far in excess of any fashionable biological or psychological emphasis that could occur in individual training. It is equally obvious that our 3,000-year-old lineal stress did not originate nor terminate in biological bias or in toilet habits.

Gertrude Stein in *The Making of Americans* sets up the anal-oral axis very naturally as the correlative of verbalization:
"I cannot remember not talking all the time and all the same feeling that while I was talking that I was not only hearing but seeing . . .
A history of anyone must be a long one, slowly it comes out from them . . . in the kind of repeating each one does."

What Freud calls "oral" is noted as typical of pre-literate societies and is applied to one by Anthony F. C. Wallace in his study of Iroquois culture (*Symposium on Local Diversity in Iroquois Culture* ed. by W. N. Fenton). Oral cultures in the auditory sense naturally have small time sense because they play by ear. And all time is *now* in oral societies. This auditory space is a physical field and its spherical character really explains the bias and expectations of oral, pre-literate societies. Likewise the visual lineality of scribal and print cultures really includes the anal-oral axis, with strong anal stress, of course. The psychodynamics of sight, sound and language take easy precedence over social biology as concepts and instruments of explanation of these phenomena.

SHERLOCK HOLMES VS THE BUREAUCRAT

10 The popular idea of Holmes, the many-sided man, and of his many triumphs over Scotland Yard is a vivid image of the basic clash of attitudes in Western culture.

Sherlock Holmes is so much the type of the intuitive genius that it is unnecessary to dwell at length on the characteristics of the intuitive mind. It is a mind for which situations are total and inclusive unities. Every facet, every item of a situation, for Holmes, has total relevance. There are no irrelevant details for him. In an organic complex all parts have total relevance, not just *some* relevance to the whole. In the nineteenth century the power of biological metaphor such as obsessed the Holmesian mind of Samuel Taylor Coleridge in his scrutiny of artistic creation, gradually was extended to every phase of human speculation and inquiry.

The concentration on biological analogy with its assumption of total relevance of the least details begins to appear in the joy taken in the new realism, in documenting the most ordinary scenes from daily life in the press, in the novel, in painting.

Flaubert worked in exactly the opposite way from his notion of *le mot juste*. For Flaubert, every word in a long novel had total relevance to the whole novel not just to the local episode. He was the first to return to contrapuntal composition in which all levels of action and implication are simultaneous and in which character becomes theme or motif. Flaubert like Holmes is an instance of the new artist for whom every art situation is total and inclusive of many of the simultaneous levels which occur in actual experience.

THE ART AND THE BUREAUCRAT

For the artist with his organic, vivisectional (or living section) point of view of man and society, the natural enemy is the bureaucrat, the man with the tidy desk, the big file, the orderly mind devoid of simultaneous modes of awareness or observation. It needs no documentation to sustain the view that the admirable administrations of Scotland Yard are hostile to the inclusive and instantaneous grasping of situations. The Yard technology is serial, segmented and circumstantial. They conclude effect from immediately preceding cause in lineal and chronological order. They do not dream of totalities or of the major relevance of details.

In the visual theories of Ruskin as in the poetic theories of Walter Pater the passionate devotion to vivid detail goes with growing awareness that all the arts approach a condition of music; for in music all parts tend to be simultaneous in the sense that narrative progress in musical composition must constantly recapitulate and unify as much as a movie. Toward the end of the last century Theodore Lipps the psychologist was to demonstrate that the single clang of a bell contained all possible sonatas and musical forms. *Anna Livia Plurabelle.*

As all kinds of information flowed from many quarters of the world in greater volume and at greater speed, so similar varieties of knowledge about the inner and outer life of man and society began to co-exist even in semi-literate minds. Biological metaphors of change and existence are necessary means of processing and unifying large bodies of data. Hippolyte Taine on one hand, Gustave Flaubert on the other, took up such biological concepts to revolutionize literary history and the novel. Taine undertook to explain the totality of literature *in* society as an organic and evolutionary process. His view of literature as an organic by-product of massive institutions and nationalisms lasted until recently as the basis for university study of vernacular literatures.

The ordinary man finds a hero in Holmes and in his numerous descendants because the bureaucrat is always putting the finger on each of us in a way which makes us feel like Kafka characters—guilty but mystified.

The Secretariat building at the U.N. is the biggest filing cabinet in the world.

11 Highly literate people are those who have been read aloud to when young? The eye does not move evenly along the line save when retarded and guided by the ear? Ineluctable modality of the visible.

There is an impression abroad that literary folk are fast readers. Wine tasters are not heavy drinkers. Literary people read slowly because they sample the complex dimensions and flavors of words and phrases. They strive for totality not lineality. They are well aware that the words on the page have to be decanted with the utmost skill. Those who imagine they read only for "content" are illusioned.

As Bartlett showed in his classic *Remembering,* an act of attention to any situation is an act of rearranging all the members of that situation. Recall is also restructuring.

Psychologists have shown that the eye does not apprehend while moving or while at rest. Rather there is a tremor while at rest which permits the encompassing of the object. The "reeling and writhing" of Lewis Carroll is close to the action of pre-typewriter reading and writing. The staccato stutter of the typewriter on the other hand is really close to the stutter that is oral speech. The typewriter is part of our oral revolution today. "Bygmeister Finnegan of the stuttering hand" is Joyce's figure of the inventor of spoken words and of architecture. The typist yatters to the script.

Today children have to have radio or gramophone playing in order to attend to visual tasks of reeling and writhing, rocking and rolling, reading and writing. The silent class-room favors only those who have been rigidly swaddled in habits of silent solitary reading. Is class-room swaddling a principal factor in juvenile delinquency? The normal environment with auditory messages carried simultaneously by different media on several levels creates new habits of attention in which the adult world is little-skilled. The fall in the level of literacy goes hand in hand with a great increase in range of oral verbalization. Literacy is the social acceptance of the monopoly of one mode of perception. It would be well to diagnose the total situation before pronouncing a general moral doom. Naturally the professional scribes make it their business to issue moral judgements on this technological change.

Legal contracts in today's business are just the minutes of the last meeting.

Oil Executive

12 In English libel law, "the greater the truth the greater the libel." The English conception of libel is aristocratic and oral, the American is written. Oral codes have no loop-holes for legal eagles. In oral codes the sanctions are total: ostracism—the duel.

In written, sanctions are lineal and metrical—the fine, the damages.

The Merchant of Venice is the dramatization of a clash between oral and written codes.

BECAUSE PRINT IS A

The

WORD

May

Oral societies have a code of honor. Charles James Fox was confronted by his tailor one morning when he was piling up gold pieces to pay a gambling debt. The tailor presented his bill. Fox explained the money was for a debt of honor. "Then," said the tailor tearing up his bill, "I make mine a debt of honor also." And Fox paid him on the spot. Even today in the American South order books are taboo.

The Boer general Krueger was quite illiterate, said Roy Campbell. He sat daily under a large tree administering justice. Two brothers presented themselves. They could not agree about the division of their patrimony. They showed him a map of the land. Krueger said to one: "You divide it." To the other: "You choose." The oral is quick, inclusive, total. It considers all aspects in a single instant.

If one were to ask any power group, a corporation or an ad agency: "If, by pressing a button in this room you could instantly achieve all your goals, would you press that button?" The answer would be "NO". This question merely transfers their operations from the written and analytic mode to the oral and simultaneous. It is the difference between the fairy wish and the Puritan will. The world of the oral wish at once reveals the moral quality of the goal.

Somebody said the nineteenth century saw the shift from the dance to the race, from inclusive symmetry to lineal anarchy.

Aristocracies are always oral in tendency, living by gossip and anecdote, games and sports. They make use of the scribe but despise him. Said the Duke of Gloucester to Edward Gibbon on the appearance of his *History*: "Another damned fat book eh, Mr. Gibbon? Scribble scribble scribble eh, Mr. Gibbon?" The use of the fox hunter said Wyndham Lewis, is to keep the business man in his place.

It is not accidental that oral countries like Spain, Italy, France, rely heavily on written legal codes. For the same cause (antithetic polarity) common law and oral tradition in England and America rely heavily on the general literacy of the Anglo-Saxon world.

Mr. Justice Jackson observed that "when the Court moved to Washington in 1800, it was provided with no books, which probably accounts for the high quality of early opinions. In five of Marshall's great opinions he cited not a single precedent."

Young lawyers today are encouraged to keep all books out of sight in their offices. "*You* are the law for your client."

In his "Roman Law and the British Empire" (in *Changing Concepts of Time*) Innis shows how it happens that in print cultures like ours lawyers tend to become legislators, whereas in oral cultures journalists enter the legislature. Innis might have added that the newspaper is essentially an oral form produced by oral types of men. The newspaper via the telegraph provides no explanations but instead an instantaneous global section.

Legal procedure in oral countries is inquisitorial, equally in Russia or France or Ireland. Written tradition favors, instead, the sifting of circumstantial evidence. Because Roman law countries are concerned with principles they attract the highest intellectual ability into the academic field, said Innis, and Roman Law countries are strong in the social sciences for this reason.

Always the totalitarian, inclusive and drastic character of the oral tradition in law and society. Always the fragmentary, loop-holed, and limited aspect of law in the written tradition.

These remarks imply no value judgements, no preferences. To distinguish the properties of these things avoids the confusion of moral clamor. Clarification permits co-existence, and resolution of conflict.

MILTON

HAD HIS DAUGHTERS

I

HAVE MY **DICTAPHONE**

13 Henry James on his death-bed called for his Remington. It was brought and the sound of its keys soothed his delirium. Dictating to a typist during the last 25 years of his life, Henry James revolutionized his prose. Dictation permitted the slow elaboration of those vast periods of *The Golden Bowl*. And dictation changed the style of Wyndham Lewis after his blindness.

Here is the early, visual Lewis:

There are torsos moving with bemused slowness on all sides; their helmet-capped testudinate heads jut this way and that. In their clockwork cadence the exhausted splash of the waves is a sound that is a cold ribbon just existing in the massive heat. The delicate surf falls with the abrupt clash of glass, section by section.

After his blindness the prose of Lewis became less pigmented, less kinesthetic. It acquired narrative ease:

> Pullman had noticed long before this that both giants had kicked off their shoes, which lay, very minute footwear, not far from where their feet were moving. Their clothes had everywhere burst asunder. But it was at this moment that with enormous splutters and gasps, they suddenly levitated . . . two vast nudities rose into the air and disappeared over the roofs. But they made their exit buttocks uppermost.

Most prominent among American representatives of the oral manner in prose is William Faulkner whose latest novel *The Town* (volume two) opens:

> I wasn't born yet so it was Cousin Gowan who was there and big enough to see and remember and tell me afterward when I was big enough for it to make sense.

The oral tradition of the South is a world in which past and present concert in a babble of chat and memories and observation and complicated kinship relations. An oral world keeps multiple blood relationships in easy acoustic focus in the same way as a pre-literate people have no trouble in managing complex word formations and inflections.
James W. Hart in *The Popular Book* notes that:

> Sharing the heritage of England's established religious beliefs, the Southerners were not embroiled in doctrinal dispute which made New Englanders import and print books. . . . As one of the Southern colonists said, they were more inclinable to read men by business and conversation than to dive into books.

The author of *Tom Sawyer* and *Huck Finn* stays in the heart of this oral world as much as the author of *Pogo*.

The new art or science which the electronic

or post-mechanical age has to invent

concerns the alchemy of social change.

14 We can no longer tolerate the irresponsibility of social trial and error. When information moves instantly to all parts of the globe it is chemically explosive. Any chain-reaction which occurs rapidly is explosive, whether in personal or social life.

President Sukarno of Indonesia spoke to the tycoons of Hollywood describing them as revolutionaries. They may have been shocked. But people who are as specialized as they are can't avoid shocks.

New ideas and new attitudes are disruptive. Today the normal movements of information have the effect of armed invasion on some culture or group. Earlier ages entertained themselves with speculation on the historical effect of Cleopatra's nose. We teeter hysterically on the consequences of rumor about President Eisenhower's viscera.

It is the normal aspect of our information-flow which is revolutionary now. The new media normalize that state of revolution which is war. Two hundred years ago it was idea and theory which disrupted the old regimes. Now it is just the packaged information which we call entertainment which transforms living conditions and basic attitudes. It is the ordinary flow of news and pictures from every quarter of the globe which rearranges our intellectual and emotional lives without either struggle or acceptance on our part.

Our present conceptions of what constitutes social cause, effect, and influence are quite unable to cope with this electronic simultaneity of conspicuous co-existence.

We have to know in advance the effect, on all the cultures of the world, of any change whatever. This is necessity not ideal. It is also a possibility. There was never a critical situation created by human ingenuity which did not contain its own solution.

The same technology which has made instantaneous information-flow a chemical danger to every culture in the world has also created the power of total re-construction and pre-construction of models of situations. For nearly a century we have employed reconstruction as historical method. Instead of *a view* of the past we simply re-create a model of it. This method began in detective fiction, and in symbolist poetry. Instead of a theory of a crime, the whole crime reconstructed. Instead of a poetic statement about an experience, the situation which is formula for that experience.

In a movie like *Richard III* by Lawrence Olivier there is expert reconstruction of an Elizabethan play and also reconstruction of the visual and textural and political period about which the play is concerned. The historical expertise of dozens of scholars led to a working model which any school-child could enjoy equally with an adult.

GEOGRAPHY AND TIME ARE NOW CAPSULATED. Our tendency has been to make possible the co-existence of all cultures and also of all pasts. But this means that we can also anticipate the effects of all our present actions and technology. What we must know in order to achieve this is the fact that the media of communication are not mere catalysts but have their own physics and chemistry which enter into every moment of social alchemy and change.

THE PHYSICS OF TYPOGRAPHIC LINEALITY HAVE DOMINATED OUR PERCEPTION

Previously Newtonian mechanics had been a closed system of perception. But we have moved swiftly beyond mechanization in this century, and mechanical metaphors are mostly irrelevant to the physics of our media and the demands which we should now make of our education. Why make the media of light fight on the side of darkened perception?

If we can no longer tolerate trial and error in modern urban and economic life, neither is the fact of traditional time-lag in educational procedure a matter for banal and cynical observation. When all kinds of information flowed slowly in a society, educational irrelevance could be corrected by self-education and by individual brilliance.

THAT WON'T WORK TODAY.

MANIFESTOS

About 1830 Lamartine pointed to the newspaper as the end of book culture.

THE BOOK ARRIVES TOO LATE

At the same time Dickens used the press as base for a new impressionist art which D. W. Griffiths and Sergei Eisenstein studied in 1920 as the foundation of movie art.

Robert Browning took the newspaper as art model for his impressionist epic *The Ring and the Book*; Mallarmé did the same in *Un Coup de Dés*. Edgar Poe, a press man and, like Shelley, a science fictioneer, correctly analysed the poetic process. Conditions of newspaper serial publication led both him and Dickens to the process of writing backwards. This means simultaneity of all parts of a composition. Simultaneity compels sharp focus on *effect* of thing made. Simultaneity is the form of the press in dealing with Earth City. Simultaneity is formula for the writing of both detective story and symbolist poem. These are derivatives (one 'low' and one "high") of the new technological culture. Simultaneity is related to telegraph, as the telegraph to math and physics.

Joyce's *Ulysses* completed the cycle of this technological art form.

LET

the sun and moon go!
let scenery take the applause of the audience!
let there be apathy under the stars!

Let nothing remain but the ashes of teachers,
artists, moralists, lawyers,
and learn'd and polite persons!

Let churches accommodate serpents, vermin,
and the corpses of those who have died
of the most filthy of diseases!

Let there be no unfashionable wisdom!
let such be scorn'd and derided
off from the earth!

Let a floating cloud in the sky —
let a wave of the sea — let growing mint,
spinach, onions, tomatoes — let these be exhibited
as shows, at a great price for admission!

Let shadows be furnished with genitals!
Let substances be deprived of their genitals! . . .

Walt Whitman, Respondez

. We shall sing the love of danger,
the habit of energy and boldness.

2. The essential elements of our poetry
shall be courage, daring and rebellion.

3. Literature has hitherto glorified
thoughtful immobility, ecstasy and sleep:
we shall extol aggressive movement,
feverish insomnia, the double
quick step, the somersault, the box on
the ear, the fisticuff . . .

F. T. Marinetti, Futuristic Manifesto

BEYOND *ACTION*
AND
REACTION

WE WOULD ESTABLISH OURSELVES

We start from opposite statements of a chosen world.
Set up violent structure of adolescent clearness
between two extremes.

We discharge ourselves on both sides.

We fight first on one side, then on the other, but
always for the SAME cause, which is neither side or
both sides and ours.

Mercenaries were always the best troops.

We are Primitive Mercenaries in the Modern World.

Our *Cause* Is NO-MAN'S.

We set Humor at Humor's throat.

Stir up Civil War among peaceful apes.

We only want Humor if it has fought like Tragedy.

We only want Tragedy if it can clench its side-muscles
like hands on its belly, and bring to the surface a
laugh like a bomb.

Wyndham Lewis, *Manifesto*

To believe that it is necessary for or conducive to art, to "Improve" life, for instance—make architecture, dress, ornament, in *better taste,* is absurd.

The artist of the modern movement is a savage (in no sense an "advanced," perfected, democratic, Futuristic individual of Mr. Marinetti's limited imagination): this enormous, jangling, journalistic, fiery desert of modern life serves him as Nature did more technically primitive man.

There is violent boredom with that feeble European-ism, abasement of the miserable "intellectual" before anything coming from Paris, Cosmopolitan sentimen-tality, which prevails in so many quarters.

Wyndham Lewis, *Blast*

FUTURISM AND MAGIC LIFE

1. The Futurist theoretician should be a Professor of Hoffman Romance, and attempt the manufacture of a perfect being.

Art merges in Life again everywhere.

Leonardo was the first Futurist, and, incidentally, an airman among Quattro Cento angels.

His Mona Lisa eloped from the Louvre like any woman.

She is back again now, smiling, with complacent reticence, as before her escapade; no one can say when she will be off once more, she possesses so much vitality.

Her olive pigment is electric, so much more so than the carnivorous Belgian bumpkins by Rubens in a neighbouring room, who, besides, are so big they could not slip about in the same subtle fashion.

Rubens IMITATED Life—borrowed the colour of its crude blood, traced the sprawling and surging of its animal hulks.

Leonardo MADE NEW BEINGS, delicate and severe, with as ambitious an intention as any ingenious mediaeval Empiric.

He multiplied in himself, too, Life's possibilities. He was not content to be as an individual Artist alone, any more than he was content with Art.

Life won him with gifts and talents.

2. In Northern Europe (Germany, Scandinavia and Russia) for the last half century, the intellectual world has developed savagely in one direction—that of Life.

His war-talk, sentous elevation and much besides,

MARINETTI picked up from NIETZCHE.

Strindberg, with his hysterical and puissant autobiographies, life-long tragic coquetry with Magic, extensive probing of female flesh and spirit, is the great Scandinavian figure best representing this tendency.

Bergson, the philosopher of Impressionism, stands for this new prescience in France.

EVERYWHERE

LIFE IS SAID

INSTEAD OF

ART

Wyndham Lewis

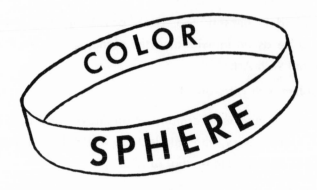

The age-old conflict between the Eastern integrity of the interval and the Western integrity of the object is being resolved in oral culture.

Pound's *Treatise on Harmony* states:

A sound of any pitch, or any combination of such sounds, may be followed by a sound of any other pitch, or any combination of such sounds, providing the time interval between them is properly gauged; and this is true for any series of sounds, chords or arpeggios.

This is a physical fact in color and in design as well.

A superimposed metronomic time or space pattern is intolerable today in verse, in town planning or in music.

Bartok sought new musical order in the rhythms and patterns of folk speech.

The interval is the means of epiphany or revelation.

It is the release which Hopkins called Sprung Rhythm.

It is the instrument of anological intuition of Being.

It is the dynamic symmetry of tensions among proportions which yields the Golden Section in space or time.

The Munsell Color Sphere does not take us into the inclusive auditory world its form implies. The spectator is left outside with one facet of color at a time.

True color experience derives from involvement of all the senses at once—synesthesia.

Man lives in such a sphere of jazzed up rag-time sensuous be-bop.

To bring order into this jangled sphere man must find its center.

A valid color sphere would have the spectator in the center.

Sensation of pure color is only possible through the acoustics of the word.

In actual visual experience of color, perception changes constantly because of factors of background and eye fatigue.

Therefore symmetrical balance and harmony are possible only when man is at the center of the sphere.

In the model sphere colors of strong hue and chroma will be at the center of the sphere, retreating colors further away.

Today our engineering and town planning permit the extension of such model spheres to every area of physical experience at ground level or from the air.

The color sphere or modulor is cued in with the auditory space of our oral, electronic culture.

THE CITY

no longer exists, except as a cultural ghost for tourists. Any highway eatery with its TV set, newspaper, and magazine is as cosmopolitan as New York or Paris.

The METROPOLIS today is a classroom; the ads are its teachers. The classroom is an obsolete detention home, a feudal dungeon.

The metropolis is OBSOLETE

ASK THE ARMY

The handwriting is on the celluloid walls of Hollywood; the Age of Writing has passed. We must invent a NEW METAPHOR, restructure our thoughts and feelings. The new media are not bridges between man and nature: they are nature.

Gutenberg made all history SIMULTANEOUS: the transportable book brought the world of the dead into the space of the gentleman's library; the telegraph brought the entire world of the living to the workman's breakfast table.

NOBODY yet knows the language inherent in the new technological culture; we are all deaf-blind mutes in terms of the new situation. Our most impressive words and thoughts betray us by referring to the previously existent, not to the present.

WE ARE BACK IN ACOUSTIC SPACE

We begin again to structure the primordial feelings and emotions from which 3000 years of literacy divorced us.

Counterblast, 1954

POETIC IMAGERY

ONLY a part of an author's imagery comes from his reading. It comes from the whole of his sensitive life since early childhood. Why, for all of us, out of all that we have heard, seen, felt, in a lifetime, do certain images recur, charged with emotion, rather than others? ...

AUDITORY

IMAGINATION

What I call the "auditory imagination" is the feeling for syllable and rhythm, penetrating far below the conscious levels of thought and feeling, invigorating every word; sinking to the most primitive and forgotten, returning to the origin and bringing something back, seeking the beginning and the end. It works through meanings, certainly or not without meanings in the ordinary sense, and fuses the old and obliterated and the trite, the current, and the new and surprising, the most ancient and the most civilized mentality.

T. S, ELIOT (From *The Use of Poetry and the Use of Criticism,* 1933)

THE WORLD OF PAPER

We take paper for granted.
We use it and forget it.
We use more than 300 pounds per person every year.
In Asia, the use of paper is less than 9 pounds a year per person.
Every scrap must be salvaged.
It must be used again and again if that is possible.
A torn magazine is a bonanza.
This is serious in the economy and progress of underdeveloped areas.

It is hard to make educational progress when paper is not available.

It is hard to hold an election if there is inadequate paper upon which to print the ballots.

New York Times, Sunday, July 7, '57

Available North American horse power per person . . **800**
Available European horse power per person **27**
Available Asian horse power per person **2**

Buckminster Fuller

We cannot pretend to think *for* others unless we think *with* them . . . "art" involves the whole of the active life, and presupposes the contemplative. The disintegration of a people's art is the destruction of their life, by which they are reduced to the proletarian status . . . in the interests of a foreign trader, whose is the *profit*.
We are proud of our museums where we display a way of living that we have made impossible.

A. K. Coomaraswamy

GAUDIER BRZESKA

The sphere is thrown through space, it is the soul and object of the vortex—

The intensity of existence had revealed to man a truth of form — his manhood was strained to the highest potential—his energy brutal—

HIS OPULENT MATURITY WAS CONVEX

Religion pushed him to the use of the

VERTICAL which inspires awe.

His gods were self made, he built them in his image, and RETAINED AS MUCH OF THE SPHERE AS COULD ROUND THE SHARPNESS OF THE PARALLELOGRAM.

IX 45

M. C. Escher

The SEMITIC VORTEX was the lust of war. The men of Elam, of Assur, of Bebel and the Kheta, the men of Armenia and those of Canaan had to slay each other cruelly for the possession of fertile valleys. Their gods sent them the vertical direction, the earth, the SPHERE.

They elevated the sphere in a splendid squatness and created the HORIZONTAL.

From Sargon to Amir-nasir-pal men built man-headed bulls in horizontal flight-wald. Men flayed their captives alive and erected howling lions: THE ELONGATED SPHERE BUTTRESSED ON FOUR COLUMNS, and their kingdoms disappeared.

THE ORGANIZATION MAN
by
WILLIAM H. WHYTE, Jr.

might well have been written as a special research assignment on the rise of oral culture in postwar America. Mr. Whyte's book says nothing explicitly of the oral theme of *Explorations 8*. His testimony to the oral swing is as involuntary as it is impressive.

15 Earlier in this issue there has been mention of the effects of print on oral societies. We call them the undeveloped areas quite properly. For technology is explicitness, and undeveloped areas are of implicitness all compact both in speech and in deed, and in raw materials.

IN

AMERICA TODAY

The Organization Man is a study of what happens when a society in which there is the most extreme application of print technology in history, suddenly swings off on the oral tack for the first time.

There is with us new insistence on long-term goals and on social security and equilibrium. There is eagerness to abandon the goals and manners of unruly enterprise in favor of those of decorous bureaucracy. There is concern to scrap the pugnacious style of individual competitive drive in favor of harmony and teamwork.

Mr. Whyte must have had an early intuition of the oral revolution because his first book was titled

IS ANYBODY LISTENING?

It was the universal experience of collective bureaucratic life in the Second War that hastened the move away from the *Ancien Regime* of individual enterprise. On page 112 Mr. Whyte remarks on the change:

At the risk of oversimplification, the difference can be described as that between the Protestant Ethic and the Social Ethic. In one type of program we will see that the primary emphasis is on work and on competition; in the other, on managing *others'* work and on co-operation.

In *How the Soviet System Works* it will be recalled that the Russian headache is to instill some "Protestant Ethic" and ruthless individual drive into a society that has been collective and feudal for many centuries. "Familyness" and the good life of easy co-operation are the bane of Soviet lineal "storm" programs.

For Mr. Whyte, we are well into a widespread offensive of collective bureaucracy which "rationalizes the organization's demands for fealty . . ." Max Weber and R. H. Tawney have made our century familiar with the theme of *Religion and the Rise of Capitalism*.

The theme of Explorations 8 is that the swing to the oral mode, individually and socially, is inevitable as soon as there is serious challenge to the monopoly of print as a means of social communication.

The classic demonstration of R. H. Tawney is how the Protestant Ethic had to fight to loosen the older social bonds exactly as the new Puritans of the Kremlin have had to fight to dissolve the older matrix. The man of print culture is necessarily a self-educated man. You can't acquire book culture by oral means. You have to struggle alone and in silence against a distracting social environment which looks askance at your solitary quest. This quest engenders psychological powers of an intensely dedicated and aggressive kind. From the point of view of the solitary quester with his inner direction and self-appointed goals and standards, it is society that is

THE LONELY CROWD

The inner-directed man of David Reisman is the man for whom the book is the transporting vehicle. Its lineal print is the railway line so abhorrent to the bureaucratic executive who relies on air travel and radar. Mr. Whyte reports a most relevant fact about the new executive (model 1957):

Similarly, while the organization encourages executives to do extensive reading of business periodicals and trade journals—often by free sub-scriptions—few executives would dream of being caught reading them in the office. Such solitary contemplation during the office day, for some reason, is regarded by even the executive himself as a form of hookey.

It follows, of course, that the truly individualist and entrepreneurial scene today is the university. Having long enjoyed a bureaucratic haven from the individualist anarchy of commerce, the university man is becoming aggressively non-conformist. His intense book training makes this easy for him. But he has previously held back out of an instinctive sense of his antithetic role. Today sparked by private grants from the big collective foundations the professor is able to function as a figure of private initiative and as an employer of labor. Today, in a word, the professor is about to assume the individualist role relinquished by the business community. Private enterprise having whirled itself into a super-bureaucratic dimension, seeks to perpetuate itself in a new collective way with long-term goals. It is prepared to use its vast funds to subsidize the very individualism which it has outgrown.

Mr. Whyte, in noting the executive neurosis of our day, says:
The real conflict, I am going to argue . . . is the conflict *within* work. Of all the organization men the true executive is the one who remains most suspicious of The Organization. If there is one thing that characterizes him, it is a fierce desire to control his own destiny and, deep down . . . he wants to dominate, not be dominated.

In short, the executive is still a product of society whose tradition is profoundly that of print technology, or "the Protestant ethic", as Max Weber and Mr. Whyte call it. But though it is painful he is sufficiently the realist to accept the new social ethic of electronic communication.

Compared to Big Business, Academic and Literary Worlds often seem like a Jungle.

"Let me add", says Mr. Whyte, "a personal testimonial on this score. . . . The corporation man is a different breed; he has obeyed the precept to team play so long it has become part of his personality. One result is often a rather automatic, and icy bonhomie, but another is a remarkable capacity to disagree with colleagues professionally without having to dislike them personally. By contrast the academic and literary worlds often seem like a jungle."

For the man of the printed word another man has to run on the same rails with himself in order to be in the same world at all. So that paradoxically, this highly specialist, lineal, individualist exacts a high degree of conformity from his fellow travellers. Whereas, the conformist—bureaucrat, accustomed to oral conference as the mode of processing his problems, is much more like the parliamentarian who freely dines with the opposition.

The backward jungle of the senior combination room. The teacher shortage today may well be due to the teacher role being far too individualist and rugged for the potential teachers of new oral society. The pastoral scene of the Little Red Schoolhouse looks like a Blackboard Jungle to the new conformists. The Second War was for most of its participants a large experience of a new kind of society based on the immediate and fullest use of our technology. Afterwards there was a decisive change of mood and attitude among the young in America. They looked longingly toward corporation life. But it should not be supposed that this was the result of the experience of army conformity or hierarchy. The key is the fact that the armed services depend without any inhibitions on the fullest use of electronic communications.

The Air Force brass meet for daily conference by closed circuit TV. The armed services had no hesitation in discarding all the traditional forms of print technology and lineal procedure. They provided a working model of the new electronic age.

So, on the one hand, Mr. Whyte observes that:

> Blood brother to the business trainee off to join Du Pont is the seminary student who will end up in the church hierarchy, the doctor headed for the corporate clinic, the physics Ph.D. in a government laboratory, the intellectual on the foundation-sponsored team project, the engineering graduate in the huge drafting room at Lockheed, the young apprentice in a Wall Street law factory.

Yet these passive young collectivists, renegades from a 300-year tradition of print-dominated culture, are not conservatives, says Mr. Whyte. Perhaps contemporaryism would be a better word than conservativism to describe their posture.

A central feature of their oral attitude appears in the view of Professor Pittenger at General Theological Seminary:

> It is a kind of authoritarianism in reverse. Theological students today, in contrast to their fellows of twenty years ago, want "to be told" . . . most anxious to have it "laid on the line".

This indeed is lineality in reverse. Since the true lineal man is eager to whirl privately and silently along the lines of type, he is the last to want to hear or share a party line of any sort. Oral structures new and old have always set up inter-locking programs whose operators are in no need of being aware of one another. This especially appears in the several inter-locking and non-communicating secret service organizations in the Soviet.

The oral man never asks for a blueprint. He never wants an over-all *view*. His but to feel he is a member of the team. The only possibility in an oral structure is a monarchical apex of control. Where the activities of many are to be orchestrated there can be only one conductor. But the more necessary the conductor the more expendable he becomes. The first job of a top executive today is to see to it that there are several who can succeed him instantly. They often do!

It is this interlocking character of oral structures so patent to Mr. Whyte in his study of corporations that has brought also into his view the unwittingly interlocking character of our society as a whole. To De Tocqueville the oral, aristocratic outsider, the unity of the American dynamic was far plainer than to the lineal-minded members of the society. Mr. Whyte is struck by the unity in our diversity today:

> Most believers in the many sub-branches of American organization-life are still unaware of the interlocking nature of their separate credos . . . change a word here and there, however, and what many an educator is prescribing is exactly what many a personnel man is prescribing, and many a research director, and so on through the roster of our institutions.

Mr. Whyte views with some alarm our oral drive toward conformity and precise, interlocking musical harmony. He has detached himself from the old matrix of print technology and culture and has seen the new forms that are taking over. Of course, had we had any awareness of the psycho-dynamics of our Gutenberg era before it began to yield to the Marconi era we would have been less surprised and much better able to effect a proper transition to the new culture without total jettisoning of the educational and social values of print and lineality. Instead of understanding these matters we have tended to substitute moral denunciation and recrimination, alarm and complacency.

Mr. Whyte is not happy about the Utopian social engineers of today who aim at total integration of man and society. He is not happy about the young corporation trainees eager to be processed into standardized entities so that they can be available as replaceable parts in a big organization:

Not Big Brother Is Watching But All The Brothers. Trainees speak frequently of the way close fraternity life atmosphere is valuable in ironing out some trainees' aberrant tendencies. It may be tough on him, they concede, but better now than later. In a few years the trainee will be released from this close association and the social character that he has perfected will be a fundamental necessity; he will be moving from one company branch to another, and he must be able to fit into the same kind of integrated social system.

In conjunction with the East India Company and the British Civil Service the English set out to produce such a product in the mid-nineteenth century. The British Public School **British Boy** Boy modelled on the gentleman-scholar of 2,000-**with Teak** year-old bureaucracy of Confucian China was **of Chan.** hastened into assembly-line production at Rugby. He lasted a century, and then proved quite unable to adapt to our new oral culture today. We may have better luck with our new trainees.

Those heading for organization life ignore their toilet training

Mr. Whyte notes that the new crop of young executives "in turning their backs on the Protestant Ethic . . . are without avarice". They are unmercenary, they don't want a million. They are serious and don't talk in terms of the dollar but of "the good life".

This life is, first of all calm and ordered . . . It is a nice place out in the suburbs, a wife and three children, one, maybe two cars . . . and a summer place up at the lake or out on the Cape, and a good college education for the children.

It is obviously impossible to live in the new electronic world with its instantaneous audio-visual contacts with everybody whatever and also to retain any idea of Robinson Crusoe existence or Walden Pond. The effect of this simultaneous awareness is understandably paralyzing to some. Mr. Whyte gives the experience of the Ford Motor Company with a big field training program for college graduates:

Somewhat like the General Electric program, it was a centralized observation-orientation program through which incoming recruits were taken on a grand tour of the Company which lasted two years . . . the program created a cadre of "crown princes" that did not gibe at all well with the organization . . . the trainees had gotten such a broad view of things that they had become quite confused as to what specifically they wanted to do in the way of actual work.

This plight of the Ford "crown princes" is in varying degree the lot of all people in our society today.

Literally everybody gets more or less the same universal awareness not of an organization but of the entire globe. The effect is to make people indifferent to work or to success, as these have been known in the past. What Mr. Whyte presents as *The Organization Man* is not the image of the future industrialist but of the man of the age that has passed beyond mechanization. The age of automation may well be not the age of the consumer but of mystic contemplation.

In Alfred Zimmern's *The Greek Commonwealth* there is a Utopian picture of Greek life which we may be about to surpass:
"The Greek need not, and does not, labour from morning to night to keep body and soul together. He has never needed and never liked sustained and monotonous activity of the kind which Northern workers and Northern economists tend to regard as the inevitable lot of all mankind. The Greek has never known what it is to be, in the common sense of the word, either in his habits or his ideals, an economic man. The Greek word for unemployment is 'scholê', which means 'leisure': while for business he has no better word than the negative 'ascholia', which means 'absence of leisure'. The hours and weeks of unemployment he regards as the best and most natural part of his life. Men who live among vines and olives fall naturally into this free and irresponsible frame of mind. Nature ripens the fruit, and man has only to wait and pick it. The Greeks always lived with a fine margin of leisure; and leisure is the mother of art and contemplation, as necessity is the mother of technical devices we call 'inventions'. The Greek peasant understood and enjoyed the depth and subtlety of Euripides, but he had never thought of so simple a contrivance as a windmill.

Our steady monotonous economic activity mostly goes on indoors, generally in cramped and sedentary postures. We do not do this from choice, but because the nature of the climate and of our work compels it. Most of us would spend all our time out of doors if we could. So would the Greeks, and there was nothing to prevent them. 'I never spend my time indoors,' says the typical Athenian in Zenophon. 'My wife is quite able to manage the household by herself,' and he went out cheerfully to spend his day in the fields, or the market-place, or the wrestling-ground, or the law-courts, or the assembly, or wherever else duty or pleasure called him. All the chief institutions of Greek life took place in the open. The Greek was seldom at home. He only used his house for sleeping and eating. You will not find him in his private garden: for a Greek city, crushed within the circuit of its walls, has no room for gardens, and what was the use of them with orchards just outside the walls? He will be at work or along with the other men in some public place."

After Madame Bovary character becomes theme again in art

structures. In all serious writing thereafter characters ceased

to be VERTICAL ENTITIES in a social milieu.

Let the reader check Eliot's "Sweeney Erect" and its epigraph for an ironic comment on this major development in the arts.

16 In Chaucer the realism never detracts from the polyphony of character themes or contrapuntal melodies all simultaneously heard. Until about 1600 in art, literature and music, the only way of organizing a structure was the song technique of superimposed or parallel themes and melodies. When the Romantics say that "Shakespeare draws his characters in the round" they are using their own flat, painterly language to describe the Shakespearean music. All of Shakespeare exists in auditory depth. He evokes and defines his world in auditory space. The complexity of any of his characters is enforced by all the others being simultaneously present. Music has the power of instantly imposing its own assumptions.

So persistent is this auditory mode in Shakespeare that he has none of the pictorial habit of Jonson or Beaumont and Fletcher in displaying character against local background. He had no fashionable sophistication. No upper class patina.

The sudden shift to painting people *in their humours*, or as dominated by a ruling passion (Don Quixote) corresponds to the sudden discovery of harmonics in musical narrative. It corresponds to Montaigne's minute portraiture of his reactions to books or to Poussin's or Breughel's sudden placing of figures *in* a landscape and not in front of it. The landscape could now function pictorially as humour or ruling passion in narrative, drama, or essay.

Paint me a cavernous waste shore

Behold her single in the field

She walks in beauty, like the night

Of cloudless climes and starry skies

The contrapuntal stacking of themes once more in an auditory song structure was back in all the arts by 1900. Joyce's *Chamber Music* is strategic in selecting the vocal art of 1600 as a prism through which to refract all the new motifs of 1900.

Chronological, lineal narrative against a social background had ended. The very "background" of Proust's Paris or Joyce's Dublin had become themes and characters themselves.

But between 1600 and 1900 the landscape had been used to define and isolate passions. Then with Baudelaire, Rimbaud and Laforgue, the interior landscape had been used to control the audience emotions directly as later in advertising. This has been Mr. Eliot's forte. It is not strange that the public should be confused by a revolution in art and technique which matches the changes in physics so exactly. But it is a change easily intelligible in the light of the drive of the past century towards the dominance of the auditory and the oral as the ruling dynamic in Western experience.

To control these developments by solemn gesture of the hebdomadal hand is our current strategy. Real control comes by study of the grammars of all the media at once.

The breakdown of contrapuntal pattern in the later sixteenth century was related to the high development of printed music. Before print, musical notation served many functions, but it made no attempt to give detailed instructions to a variety of voices or instruments. And just as detailed instructions brought improvisation to an end, so in literary art there was a rapid withdrawal from contrapuntal organization.

All those aspects of recurrent Elizabethan imagery and double-plots which have been such exciting discoveries for this century, were for long the normal song and music components of verbal composition.

With the change to harmonic, vertical structure the problem was how to narrate. A century of essays ensued before the simple idea of the novel took over. Thereafter, characters held in a single passion or humor could be set on a lineal road of adventure.

THE LITURGICAL REVIVAL

17 In the later nineteenth century the artistic consciousness of those in the Arts turned towards the restoration of ritual to the whole of life.

"As for Living our Servants can do that for us." It is easy to see now that increased awareness of other and more ancient civilizations as well as interest in our own pre-industrial history, made this change a natural one. Excited sentiment was also evoked by closer knowledge of primitive societies. As Tom Harrisson explains in *Savage Civilisation* (London, Gollancz, 1937)

> There is no artistic native or great artist or respect for art: because all are artists and their art is an essential branch of their green uniform tree. . . . No man is unable to carve, dance and tell stories.

> The impulse to art form is tradition via ritual (and religion). The object of art form is the satisfaction of ritual; and the intensification of life beyond mere necessity into beauty, fury or ecstasy. In these Borneo tribes as in all pre-literate societies: creative art is very rare; tradition dominates this part of life as it dominates all parts. In any tribe the war clubs, for example, are of only two or three types. One of the commonest has four knobs at the end, always and only four knobs; not three knobs or five knobs. No man would consider the making of other than four. . . . Intangible things co-operate in every effort of making, from human conception to canoe building. A man does not carve a bird figure; he partakes in the carving.

Always the key to oral culture, primitive or model 1957, is the stress on participation, on creative passivity. It is the twentieth-century consumer attitude which has given such great retrospective stress to Keats's "negative capability" and to T. S. Eliot's "catalyst" concept of creativity.

Why should we only toil, the roof and crown of things? As our consumer role increased from our industrial output we became sympathetically aware of all the passive cultures and concepts.

No one who has looked at the matter has ever underestimated the decisive change brought about in the Christian ritual by the advent of print. Every history of the Reformation and the Renaissance insists on this. But the matter has not been considered in respect to the psychodynamics of print, any more than it is recognized that today from many directions we are returning to collective liturgical participation because of the oral bias of our new electronic culture.

In his *Liturgical Piety* (University of Notre Dame Press, 1955) Father Louis Bouyer cites a conversation between Cranmer and Gardiner which occurred while both were still Catholic priests.

A Conversation in Early Gutenberg Period. Cranmer said, "How sad it is that the people in the nave of the church do not understand anything about what is being celebrated in the sanctuary!" And Gardiner answered, "Don't worry about that, it has never occurred to them that they might want to understand it." How distressing it is for us now to consider that it was the future heretic who had the more truly Catholic reaction!"

In *The Reformation in England* (London, Hollis & Carter, vol. II, p. 89) Father Hughes cites Gardiner at length on the mode of assisting at Mass in earlier periods:

And therefore it was never meant that people should indeed hear the Mattins or hear the Mass, but be present there and pray themselves in silence. . . . And I have known that, after their little devotions said, as they called them, some used to gather by the penny or two pence such money as they had lent in gross. But as for hearing of Mass in deed, some, well occupied, heard not, and some, evil occupied, heard not neither.

Gardiner speaks out of the oral tradition of the earlier age and is utterly baffled by the urgently pressed claims of many avant-gardists like Cranmer. What Cranmer meant, as we can see in retrospect, was that people were now reading privately and wanted to follow the Mass congregationally with their texts.

For the same reason today literate people don't want to follow just the text of the Mass but want the dialogue Mass. The new oral culture of the West has created an entirely new situation liturgically. The sensibilities of literate people are rapidly shifting into new auditory preference. Sensibility is inclusive and precedes analytic awareness. But the oral culture of the Middle Ages (as of the Latin world today) isolated the worshipper at Mass. Print created a closely knit congregationalism on one hand, an intense meditative and aggressive individualism on the other.

Sixteenth-century Europe was quite unable or unwilling to understand the psycho-dynamics of these totally new conditions of culture. The Jesuits were the first to establish a form of education which took the individualist and militant aspect of print into account. Correlatively they were enthusiastic for the spectacular and visual quality of liturgy which we know as the "Baroque" in which the congregation becomes spectator. As Father Bouyer says of the anecdotal and picturesque Baroque Mass:

Key Role of the JESUITS

As if the liturgy were aiming at reproducing materially and theatrically the acts by which we were saved. . . .

The very idea of a single audience looking at a single scene or action through a proscenium arch, so typical of the Renaissance, so unmedieval, is the pure projection of the form of the printed page into drama. The dramatic unities naturally become a serious problem for spectators of such an easel-painting world. By contrast the medieval stress was for cycle plays simultaneously performed as at a circus.

That dissociation of sensibility which Mr. Eliot notes as typical of the Renaissance is much more obvious in liturgy and ritual under the impact of print. The printed word made every reader Pope, Priest and King in his private silent world. Today the liturgists would retain this with qualifications. As we move once more into an oral, passive, and collectivist attitude, the Protestant world is abandoning its Bible-reading and the Catholic liturgists are exhorting the Catholic community to undertake the scriptural quest which the Protestants are relinquishing. Father Bouyer points to the Scriptures as the indispensable corollory of liturgical piety:

This means that the first and fundamental condition for any liturgical revival which is truly a revival of piety must be a personal knowledge of the whole Bible and meditation on it, both to be achieved along lines laid out for us by the liturgy.

This, of course, is antithetic to any lineal attitude to Scripture as a stenographic record of Divine dictation.

Any observation of the many-levelled move towards oral culture in our time could not avoid mention of liturgical revivals. These revivals have been as misunderstood as the "daily-life-as-art-and-ritual" movements of the mauve decade.

HOW ABOUT WINE

18 It is supreme in oral societies. It yields to hard liquor in industrial
societies when dissociation of sensibility sets in? Wines have hard
going in a literary society because their first appeals are sensory and
direct. This appeal is hard to spell out, but becomes a challenge to the
literary. So the idea of wines, their social aura is rarified and intellectualized. Wines then become something to talk about but not to drink.

Captured by the literary lasso, wines go the way of

being talked about but never consumed.

A wine dinner is a social situation where peole are gradually exhilarated, their tongues L O O S E N E D, their response to others quickened, and their exchanges flow easily. A usual comment at a wine dinner is that "everybody is so nice tonight". Hard liquor is grimly sociable, not agreeably social, and is drunk for the effect. The effect is to release tensions, to get a load on, to have a good time, to laugh it up. The wallop is the important thing, not the experience of drinking. With wines, the pleasure is in the drinking, in the t o t a l experience.

WINES ARE POPULAR WHEN PEOPLE ARE EBULLIENT

UP and *DOING*—

ALL OVER THE ANCIENT WORLD DURING THE

DARK OR VIVID

AGES

DURING THE AGE OF EXPLORATION

AND DURING THE

VICTORIAN ERA

Hard liquor is popular when people are down and waiting; immediately before and after the sixteenth century, during the Romantic and Edwardian periods in England, and between the wars in America. Wine drinking was popular in the United States when the Republic was being formed, when the west was being opened up, AND TODAY!

We have redis- covered the meaning of "a corking good time"?

What is happening today is that the literary person, who continues to talk about wines, is being by-passed or ignored. People are simply beginning to pull corks to find out for themselves, although many still resist their curiosities and instincts as a reaction to the literary.

Wine has a shorthand language (BODY, BOU-QUET) much of which is French (SÈVE, MACHÉ, MORDANT) that is irritating and and often literary-sounding, but which is precise in meaning even when a definition is subtle and complex. BODY, for instance, is simply wateriness; BOUQUET is the collection of smells; SÈVE is sappiness; MACHÉ is the quality of coating your teeth the way spinach does; and MORDANT is descriptive of a quality of being able to bite or chew a wine. But these meanings are only simple when apprehended directly; they are tasted easily but not quite comprehensible with tasting.

This shorthand language was originally a market-place language, needed to transmit information to simplify buying and selling and to reach a price. These workmanlike terms came over naturally into the vocabulary for appreciating wines. But basically, wine knowledge is handed down orally. WINE MAKERS COMMUNICATE MORE WITH NODS, WINKS, SHRUGS, AND FACIAL GESTURES than with words, describing one wine in terms of a previous batch or vintage, perhaps never tasted but described by a grandfather repeating the description by gesture as told to him by his grandfather. I have heard, for instance, a description of the wines of 1811, so that I know them when I check my written notes. (These notes list similar vintages and include descriptive words, but when I look at them, I have a mental picture of the man who described the wine as his father described it to him.) This is valid wine knowledge, almost completely oral and visual. In this way wines long gone are still alive. Like music and poetry, wine has the power of instantly imposing its own assumptions.

Wines cannot be intellectualized well. Almost all wine writing that is not descriptive of the country or the people is bad, and even the best writing about wine itself is in terms of its effect. Chaucer talks about being transported to Spain by a glass of sherry and Falstaff describes the effect of sherry on himself. But these are descriptions of the sensations and the sensory images evoked by wine, not descriptions of wine itself.

You drink wines, and you can only describe wine well when you are talking to someone, face to face, who is also drinking the wine.

Wine cannot be part of a literary world because tasting and drinking are simultaneous. A sip is very complex: as you raise the glass to your lips you take a slight breath, inhaling the smell of the wine as you taste it and feel it in the mouth. Three senses are reporting at once. Because wine is volatile and is a complex collection of tastes, the whole sensation is changing as the wine first touches your mouth, as it moves to your throat, as you swallow, and as the three senses recover from the action. It is interesting that the ears shut off as you swallow, helping you to focus on the working senses, and that your eyes seem to cease to focus as you taste, although there may be a recalled image of the way the wine looks or of the surroundings. At the same time, various muscle senses are involved in tasting and swallowing, for instance, the grimace when you taste of something sour; this muscle reaction is recognizable when exaggerated to the point of unpleasantness, but is almost unnoticed when a normal part of the taste. A description of tasting wine is also inhibited by the few words existing to describe taste sensations, a fact in itself that is proof of the non-literary character of wine drinking.

The taste of any good wine is an essence, and it is possible to describe it, but many words are needed. Wine is also complex, and an old wine will contain perhaps twenty different alcohols and a collection of other constituents, many of which change as the wine comes in contact with the air and with the drinker's tasting gear. The bottle would be long gone before wordifying would be complete.

A taster is lost when he starts thinking about the wine he has just sipped. His task is to recognize what is happening to him; usually the attempt to verbalize his sip drives this out of his consciousness.

The most successful book on wines published in America, for instance, is essentially a listing of vineyards and wine names and words. Doctors and medical people are America's largest group of fine wine lovers, perhaps because they are too busy for all but the simple pleasures that can be made part of the normal routine of eating and drinking.

TELEVISION MURDERS TELEPHONY IN BROTHER'S BROIL

Anna was, Livia is, and Plurabelle's to be

FINNEGANS WAKE

19 The bell and/or the belle is/are simultaneously all things. The age of the electronic and the simultaneous is to be an age of bell(es).

Joyce gives the history of human culture and of man's fallen state in a single phrase:

"BALBUS WAS BUILDING A WALL."

The youthful Stephen Dedalus meditated on this phrase from his Latin grammar.

On the second page of *Finnegans Wake* his meditation on this theme has expanded to include the development of all speech and architecture:
Offwhile balbulous, mithre ahead, with goodly trowel in grasp and ivoroiled overalls which he habitacularly fondseed, like Haroun Childeric Eggeberth he would caligulate by multiplicables the alltitude and malltitude until he seesaw by neatlightof the liquor wheretwin 'twas born, his roundhead staple of other days to rise in undress maisonry upstanded (joygrantit!), a waalworth of a skyerscape of most eyeful howth entowerly, erigenating from next to nothing and celescalating the himals and all, hierarchetectitiptitoploftical, with a burning bush abob off its baubletop and with larrons o'toolers cluttering up and tombles a' buckets clattering down.

Which is to say, when bulbous begins to build a wall then Humpty Dumpty has decided to have a great fall.

When the spherical word tries to become the lineal brick then the language stutters "entowerly".

Even spoken words are a kind of stuttering. A word is an auditory spatial unit arresting and defining a movement of thought. When the auditory unit is given a visual or written translation it becomes much more brick-like. It is then that all the king's horses and all the king's men begin their bureaucratic struggle to reassemble Humpty Dumpty, the violated word. Can that which bureaucratic and analytic means find it impossible to achieve now be done electronically?

The multi-billioned relations of the atoms in a cubic centimeter of matter can be reported for any given instant by electronic computer. This complex piece of information is recorded as a single curve.

Does all architecture originate in the bulbous dome and the beehive hut dear to oral societies? Is the tale of the tribe the tale of a tub?

Is the dimaxion igloo of Buckminster Fuller another evidence of the drive of our electronic technology toward auditory spatial form?

Perhaps Humpty Dumpty, the shattered word, can be heard once more, can be reassembled electronically?—the ineluctable modality of the audible, plurabelle's to be.

A bell is to auditory space what a polished surface is to a visual space— a mirror. ALP is river mirror of HCE the mountain. It is he for whom the belles toil.

They toil to restore him to life, the life of unified and inclusive consciousness. Till he wakes to that life the artist attempts artificial respiration.

SPICKSPOOKSPOKESMAN

OF OUR

SPECTURESQUE SILENTIOUSNESS!

PEOPLE OF THE WORD

20 Let us repeat what we were about to say:

In *The Two-Edged Sword* (Bruce Publishing Co., Milwaukee, 1956) John L. McKenzie S.J. shows how Biblical studies in the twentieth century have abandoned the concept of lineal stenographic inspiration. Since the prophet was the very antithesis of the scribe, it was absurd to think of him as waiting for words to be set down in a line. This notion derived from literary cultures led to regarding the Bible as a sort of dictionary. Our own return to oral culture in the twentieth century has enabled us to see that the prophet as divine instrument was totally so. Not only his pen but his whole being and his whose culture was the instrument for recording the voice of the Lord:

Modern control and use of natural forces was not known to the Hebrews, nor did the wildest fancy dream of anything like it . . . the ancient Hebrews were prephilosophical; the most ordinary patterns of modern thought were unknown to them. Logic as a form of mental discipline, they lacked. Their language is the speech of the simple man who sees motion and action rather than static reality. static reality as concrete rather than abstract. It prefers nouns to adjectives for it does not even like to make the obvious distinction between a substance and its properties. It sees reality rather as it is sensible than as it is intellectually apprehended, in its large outlines and in its superficial and palpable qualities. The sentences of the Hebrew are simple statements of subject and predicate, following one another with subordination; for the Hebrew looked on all propositions as having much the same weight, and rarely attempted that precise statement of the interrelation of propositions which is expressed by grammatical subordination. The

The mouth of the just shall meditate wisdom, and his tongue shall speak judgement.
Psalm xxxvi, 30–31.

language is repetitive, for repetition is almost the only form of argument and emphasis which the Hebrew knew. Johannes Pedersen has said that thinking for the Hebrews was "to grasp a totality; for the modern man, thinking is rather an analysis of a totality."

Antithetic to this oral habit of total awareness is the outlook of the scribe.

CAREFUL,
CALCULATING,
METICULOUS,

the sage or the scribe is an individualist.

The figure of the sage long pre-dates any of the books of the Old Testament. The wisdom of the sage appears in the conduct of life and the prudent management of private affairs. "The scribes were the eyes, the ears, the memory, the hands of the men who guided the destinies of Egypt." They had to be wise. They accumulated a great store of maxims which were memorized in the scribal schools. They were analytical, fragmentary, segmented in their outlook. But not to any degree approaching the outlook of those produced by printed culture.

ALL MEN ARE BORN EITHER PLATONISTS OR ARISTOTELIANS, said Coleridge. The aristocratic Plato had a low opinion of scribes and stenographers, yet his world of ideas is almost entirely visual. Whereas Aristotle, the man of method and scribal order, appeals in his philosophy entirely to the ear. His philosophy has no visual effects at all. Plato is paradoxically the darling of literary men, Aristotle of oral, intuitive men. The man of the written dialogue finally assumes a literary role.

In the age-old history of the conflict between written and oral temperaments or traditions there is no more dramatic episode than Churchill's shaking his fist under the nose of General Brooke his Chief of Staff: "I do not want any of your long-term projects, they cripple initiative!"

Let us compare Father McKenzie's account of Hebrew narrative on p. 64 of the *Two-Edged Sword* with the normal native method in an oral society:

> So much may be said to explain that the story of the Hebrews is not history as we understand the word. Now we must turn our attention to the singular character of the Hebrew story, the character which makes it unparalleled in the literature of the ancient Near East. The story, as such, is a detached item; the memory preserves incidents, and does not retain the past in a long consecutive account. The story-teller collects these incidents, but neither does the storyteller weave

them into a consecutive account; he groups the incidents in "cycles", as they are called, revolving about an individual person, a particular group, a place. The stories thus assembled have no inner connection with each other, and they do not always fit neatly when they are put together; but this does not bother the storyteller. There are two incidents reported in which David met Saul for the first time, a story which must have been often told; but David can have met Saul for the first time only once. The Hebrew stories also are a collection of detached incidents; it is the higher unity into which they are woven that sets them off from other collections of oral traditions.

And here is Tom Harrisson's account of native story-telling in *Savage Civilisation* (p. 352):

Songs are a form of story-telling. Words are a native art with an intricate circular pattern. The lay-out and content in the thousand myths which every child learns (often word perfect, and one story may last hours) are a whole library. While every incident in daily life can form a story. Any native may tell you, for a couple of hours, about how Taveta tried to steal Karai's woman. He will describe exactly how the missionary came, he picked up a piece of orange peel, just here, he held it in two fingers, these fingers, so, talking, there, and he said the following words. . . . And his right foot was against the far side of the root, just out of sunlight, the left foot was wearing a groove as deep as a thumb nail, he seemed to be nervous; some hairs, grey ones, were over his ears, etc., etc., on and on, incredible observation and detail—yet so well done that it does not get boring, the hearers are held in a web of spun words.

Father McKenzie introduces another central aspect of oral tradition which had felt the transformation of writing even before Abraham:

. . . But to the Hebrews, faith in the Lord was never a matter of assimilating a body of truth, but of surrender to a person. Even in such phrases as instruction and the word of the Lord, they had no notion of redeeming the nations from ignorance. Their prophets were not teachers. When Alexander conquered the ancient Semitic world, he saw himself as a missionary carrying Greek civilization, with its literature, art, philosophy, and vices, into the darkness of the ignorant heathen world, and he succeeded even more than he had dreamed. The Hebrews had nothing of this sort to offer, and not until they came in touch with the Greek world and Greek learning did they begin to think themselves possessed of a message for the mind. The kingdom was not a constitution, not a legal system, not a civilization, not a philosophy, not a political form; it was the realized will of the Lord imposed upon mankind, and a regeneration of the cosmos and of human nature. This could be accomplished only by the Lord Himself, and

He is the agent of the final revolution, as Hebrew prophecy depicts it. And in view of the evidence of that "collectivism" which seems inseparable from the oral, a final note on the Hebrew mode of awareness:

The religious history of the Hebrew people from its origins to its final catastrophe is the history of a collective personality; the prophets commonly imagine Israel as an individual, and address Israel as an individual.

CHURCHILL ${}_{M}{}^{O}\,{}^{Z}_{B}\,{}_{L}^{I}{}^{S}_{I}\,{}^{E}$ mobilizes

THE ENGLISH LANGUAGE

21 Beverly Nichols records:
During the darkest days of the war when Sir Winston Churchill was almost literally fighting the entire battle with his voice, I wrote: "We had nothing to fight with but words; Churchill mobilized the English language."

If ever there were a public person of oral temper and character it is Churchill. But the full significance of this oral man only becomes vivid and stark when set off against the methodical, lineal temper of his chief of staff, Lord Alanbrooke.

Arthur Bryant's *The Turn of the Tide* "based on the War Diaries of Field Marshal Viscount Alanbrooke" (Collins, London, 1957) is as complete a picture of the British clash of written and oral men as William Whyte's *The Organization Man* is a picture of the same clash in America. Bryant sets up the contrast between the two men right off:

Yet, if the palm for courage and constancy in the struggle against Hitler belongs to Churchill, that for far-sighted strategy may well be awarded by posterity to Alanbrooke.

Bird-watcher Alanbrooke tells the story of Churchill's casual decision to change destination just at take-off time and notes:

He loved these sudden changes of plans. Unfortunately he often wished to carry out similar sudden changes in strategy. I had the greatest difficulty in making him realize that strategy was a long-term process in which you could not frequently change your mind.

Here is the same paradox that appears in *How the Soviet System Works* (Bauer, Inkeles, Kluckohn), that an oral society exhibits the most arbitrary shifts of pattern in short-run policy, and at the same time the utmost inflexibility of pattern and purpose in the long run.

Churchill, for whom the whole English language was as much a simultaneous entity as all facets of the war, could act optimistically and whimsically at all times. The long-term meant unchanging confidence and resourcefulness within, and an outer readiness to do everything at once.

CHURCHILL

ALANBROOKE

Churchill was inflexible on a total basis; but his chief of staff for whom there could be only one goal or task at a time was as pessimistic as he was meticulous and methodical. For Alanbrooke the long-term process meant the systematic pursuit of a single line. Alanbrooke was inflexible on a segment.

When Alanbrooke discussed strategy with the Americans he was baffled by their preference for global strategy:

> . . . again discussion of global strategy which led us nowhere. The trouble is that the American mind likes proceeding from the general to the particular whilst in the problems we have to solve we cannot evolve any sort of general doctrine until we have carefully examined the particular details of each problem.

As soon as he encountered the Americans, Alanbrooke became an oral man by contrast. In his own British and oral culture he was an extreme example of the lineal bureaucrat. But as soon as he met the men of a Simon-pure print culture with their yen for blue-prints and over-all *pictures*, Alanbrooke rallied to the oral pole of his own culture. The Americans as visual, lineal men had to begin from the total *scene* before they could proceed to small local analysis. Whereas the man of British oral background always has the auditory sense of being in possession of the whole situation and is ready to consider only particulars. Even the Canadian has some of this auditory sense of the over-all as something felt rather than as something spelt-out or visualized. The auditory position always *feels* very superior to the visual one simply because of its instant, intuitive dynamic.

By contrast with England, Ireland is extremely an oral culture. Reviewing Lady Gregory's *Poets and Dreamers*, Young Joyce remarks:

> Out of the material and spiritual battle which has gone so hardly with her, Ireland has emerged with many memories of beliefs, and with one belief—a belief in the incurable ignobility of the forces that have overcome her.

Such is the belief of every oral society overcome by a methodical, written culture. Such, for example, is the belief of the American South, and such was the feeling of the ancient Hebrews toward the Egyptians. Alanbrooke experienced all the frustration of being an overpowered antithesis in his relation with Churchill: "And Winston? Thinks one thing at one moment and another the next moment . . . wants to carry out all operations simultaneously . . ." Alanbrooke underwent rapid fluctuations of mood while maintaining inflexibility of immediate manner and purpose. Churchill experienced no variety of mood but expressed the most flighty notions and rapid change of *immediate* purposes:
. . . he shook his fist in my face saying, "I do not want any of your long-term projects, they cripple initiative!" I agreed that they did hamper initiative, but told him that I could not look upon knowing where our next step was going as constituting a long-term project. I told him he must know where he was going, to which he replied that he did not want to know.

How could the written-oral clash be more sharply portrayed?

Fortunately for Churchill, Roosevelt was also a man of oral simultaneity and not of the careful, cautious, canny temper. As a clean-desk bureaucrat Alanbrooke was amazed:
The President's writing-table always interests me owing to the congestion on it. I tried to memorize the queer collection: blue vase lamp, two frames, bronze bust of Mrs. R., bronze ship's steering-wheel clock, four cloth toy donkeys, one tin toy motor-car, one small donkey made of two hazel nuts . . . plus many other articles that I cannot remember. Most of the donkeys have been there since I was in Washington last July.

Alanbrooke was noted as an example of regular hours in spite of staying up late with Churchill: "He was abstemious, quick, tidy, and exact . . . even in the greatest press he remained calm and unruffled." These are the qualities which rouse the contempt of the oral man. Churchill preferred to work by intuition and by impulse.

Churchill's mind "interested in everything pertaining to the human lot, cast a searchlight into every cranny of the nation's life". And he was "constitutionally incapable of not intervening with his entire heart, soul, and mind in any operation, great or small, of which he had cognizance". In the small morning hours when all good bureaucrats and executives are abed there poured from Churchill "a never-ending stream of ideas, projects, questionings, information, anecdotes and commentary on life and human nature".

The oral man knows nothing of that minute rationing and husbanding of energy, time and resources that besets the unwitting victim of print technology. That race of petty calculators, which Burke noticed had supplanted the gentry and honor of Europe in the eighteenth century, was as much the effect of the spread of print technology as the new organization men of today are the unwitting followers of the electronic revolution.

EMINENT EXTRAPOLATORS

The Scholastic philosophy ended very soon after print appeared.

22 SCHOLASTIC = scholia = game, leisure
SCHOLIA = school = (game, leisure?)
LUDUS LITERARIUS = Grammar school = literary game.

Scholastic was an oral technique for processing and commenting on patristic and other written texts. That is why it is becoming popular again today. The "new criticism" is not improperly labelled "scholastic" insofar as it is a technique of commenting on printed texts modelled on the flexibility of classroom discussion.

Scholasticism was a means of digesting every kind of text and of seeing it swiftly from many points of view. Print had no use for such diversity or simultaneity. Print preferred to pursue one level, one line at a time. Perhaps this is what was meant by "literal interpretation" in the sixteenth century. In the thirteenth century the literal level was held to include all levels. Three hundred years later the literal meant one level only: the level the reader happened to be on as he toured over the new macadam provided by mass-produced type. Printing was evidently the first mechanization of an ancient handicraft.

To the first age of print the oral speed of scholastic philosophy suddenly became an intolerable burden of "words, words, words". An oral culture always seems noisy and comical to a literary society.

By 1900 it appeared quite obvious that philosophy had become entirely written philosophy—philosophy about philosophy. Existentialism has ended that phase.

Introducing Ludwig Wittgenstein, Professor Morton White says that explaining his meaning is less like expounding a straightforward philosophical text and more like explaining just why or how a conversation with an understanding wife, lover, friend, or psychiatrist relieves anxiety. Quite apart from the philosophical respectability of such a new phase, nobody is likely to question its strongly oral character.

In his preface to his *Philosophical Investigations* Wittgenstein laments the fragmentary and discontinuous character imposed by philosophical honesty today: "And this was, of course, connected with the very nature of the investigation. For this compels us to travel over a wide field of thought criss-cross in every direction. The philosophical remarks in this book are, as it were, a number of sketches of landscapes which were made in the course of these long and involved journeyings."

If one were impressed by these journeys of Ludwig Wittgenstein it would be easy to point out how necessary it is for anybody today to pursue the same jet-like tour of the auditory sphere. All that need be said is that Wittgenstein is here trying to explain the character of oral as opposed to written philosophy. He asks plaintively:

But what does using one sentence in contrast with others consist in?
Do the others, perhaps, hover before one's mind? *All* of them?

From this purely auditory prospect Ludwig recoils in mock horror. He knows where to draw the line:

All of them? And *while* one is saying the one sentence, or before, or afterwards?—NO. . . . Someone who did not understand our language, a foreigner, who had fairly often heard someone giving the order "Bring me a slab!" might believe that this whole series of sounds was one word corresponding perhaps to the word for "building-stone" in his language.

Obviously Wittgenstein was a great leg-puller. He knew how to provide auditory philosophical thrills for literary philosophers. And then just when the sheer fright of the thing was getting too much he knew how to scurry back from the precipice holding his reader's hand.

If anyone has any doubts about the terrors which the written and the oral modes hold for modern philosophers let him hurry to sample Wittgenstein and the large school of logical positivists who cut each other to bits with negatives. As Ludwig puts it:

But didn't I already intend the whole construction of the sentence (for example) at the beginning? So surely it already existed in my mind before I said it out loud!—If it was in my mind, still it would not normally be there in some different word order. But here we are constructing a misleading picture of "intending", that is, of the use of the word.

There is no temptation on the part of the Wittgensteins to plough any long straight verbal furrows. They live in a quiver of simultaneity and of auditory intention.

THE OLD NEW RICH

AND

THE NEW NEW RICH

23 In his *Company Manners* Louis Kronenberger describes how "one very real social phenomenon of our time is that 'creative' people constitute America's newest *nouveaux riches*". Spectorsky in his *Exurbanites* refers to them as the symbol-manipulators, meaning those who have mastered the grammar and rhetoric of the new media.

Well, this large group, to be found in New York and Hollywood, is made up of Madison Avenue editors, publishers, public-relations men, actors, script-writers, composers, designers, consultants and the like "who earn more—usually a great deal more—than, say, $75,000 a year". Mr. Kronenberger is quite correct in saying also that nothing like these power groups of creative people ever happened before in the world.

These people are the masters of the electronic media. They have a simultaneous relation with 50 million people whereas movie stars had no such range or speed.

Asked to sing at a dinner party by Mrs. Frick, Enrico Caruso said: "My fee will be $50,000." A little abashed Mrs. Frick sought to cut him down to size by saying "Of course you would not be expected to mingle with my guests." "In that case," replied the tenor, "my fee would be only 25,000." No such irony would be possible at the expense of the new New Rich. They are not only literate but much at home in all the arts and with artists. Culture of the electronic age knows none of the old compartments of the industrial era with its Carnegies and Mellons, propped up by the virtuosity of a Duveen.

The new plutocracy of talent no longer sings for its supper at the Frick residence. Instead it deigns to invite the old New Rich to its penthouse or country home.

There is nothing either edifying or discreditable in this amusing reversal. It is mentioned here as evidence of how the new oral culture knows no specialism either of talent, class or wealth. It is an all-in affair and many wish it were all over.

NO UPSIDE DOWN

IN ESKIMO ART

24 Everybody has heard reports about the amazing powers of natives to master at once some intricate piece of mechanism. The Eskimos have proved to be wizard jet mechanics without benefit of any training whatever. These mechanisms they grasp by ear, inclusively, not by eye, analytically.

There are such people in our own society who are thoroughly confused by the three R's and rated as sub-normal until they happen to find a field for themselves. Churchill was a flop at Harrow.

The oral man cannot be trained by scribal and bureaucratic procedures. He has to have the total, simultaneous training common to aristocratic and primitive societies.

In *Explorations* 5 E. S. Carpenter reported concerning "Eskimo space concepts" their mechanical skill and their power of accurate mapping of islands whose shores had not been seen but where the sound of water alone gave them the contour. Moreover:

Aivilik artists do not confine themselves to the reproduction of what can actually be seen in a given moment from a single vantage point, but they twist and tilt the various possible visual aspects until they fully explain the object they wish to represent. They may draw a tent from one side and include, as well, an end view of the tent in order to show its shape.

Lineal perspective is, of course, absent, as from recent art which has also attempted an inclusive vision.

In *Explorations* 6 Siegfried Giedion discussed "Space Conception in Prehistoric Art", "one of the most important chapters in my forthcoming study on *The Continuity of the Human Spirit*".

What is it that separates us from other periods? What is it that, after having been suppressed and driven into the unconscious for long periods of time, is now reappearing in the imagination of contemporary artists?

The answer of *Explorations 8* to that query is simply that after thousands of years of written processing of human experience, the instantaneous omnipresence of electronically processed information has hoicked us out of these age-old patterns into an auditory world. To say this is not to take one's stand on Dixie Land. It is not to take a stand at all. It is to try to look at the entire new situation on its own terms—the necessary preliminary for any kind of realistic action. The alternative to such appraisal is *reaction*. Most response to challenging situations takes the form of attitudes of like or dislike, alarm or satisfaction. What could be a more dangerous preparation for a strategy of culture?

Every headache is the attempt of a creative idea to get born. Every problematic situation is charged with its own solution. That is why it is necessary to consult the new situation very carefully. The help will not be found in the old situation. But the old set-up may be saved by an understanding of the new one.

Giedion has re-studied the whole question of *Prehistoric Cave Paintings*. In a word, he presents the view that the cave paintings do not exist in visual space at all:

> These caverns possess no space in our meaning of this word, for in them perpetual darkness reigns . . . In these cases it is clear that prehistoric man was more anxious to hide his artistic creations than to expose them . . . The tradition of secreting the most sacred manifestations in places accessible only to the initiated persisted in the Egyptian temples . . .

Something comparable might be achieved today if paintings were shipped in dark sealed trains across the country accompanied by announcements that:

NEW ART ARRIVES TO LOOK AT AMERICA

Giedion shows how the cave painters avoided flat surfaces:
> This multiformity of the surfaces, their infinite freedom of direction and perpetual change, is at the basis of all primeval art. . . . It would . . . have been possible to select vertical and horizontal planes. But this was never done.

The cave painters were men of auditory space who modelled and choreographed their images in all dimensions simultaneously. They would have found our jet age as easy to grasp as the Eskimo does a jet engine.

A BRIDGE IN TIME

An attempt at non-euclidean aesthetics

Kirchner and Franz Marc called it *die Bruecke*. And possibly here again is an example of the "curious prophetic insight of the artist". For while *die Bruecke* was one of many splinter groups of German Expressionist painters in the Twenties, a "Bruecke", a bridge was slowly being built. The most revolutionary subject affecting European designer-artists since the early part of the present century was machine technology. It was a discovery of the beauty of the machine, and in those related functional forms of our industrial civilization as the skyscraper and the automobile —a beauty of polished and smoothly working parts which came to symbolize for a number of painters and sculptors, and even more for the architects, the distinctive qualities of our modern age. But to the more verbal culture of Europe, the acceptance of the machine-object, the substitution of auto for Aphrodite, skyscraper for Scylla, necessitated a highly oral, myth-generating mechanism, the erection of a poetic bridge to ease understanding of technological constructs.

The worship of the machine for its own sake was first promulgated by the Italian *Futurists* (Balla, Boccioni etc.) whose manifestos of 1909 and 1910 exalted the speed and impersonal power of the train, the airplane and the automobile, and whose paintings and sculptures attempted to capture the motion and force of these.

A SPEEDING AUTOMOBILE

is more beautiful than the

VICTORY OF SAMOTHRACE

It was, however, the abstract design of the machine, rather than its dynamism, which appealed to the largest group of artists, particularly those like Leger and the *Cubists* in France, Belling in Germany, Cizek's *Kinetismus* group in Vienna, Wyndham Lewis's *Vorticists* and the Russian *Suprematists* and *Constructivists* under Pevsner and Gabo.

1

"WE DENY VOLUME AS AN EXPRESSION OF SPACE. SPACE IN A TECHNIC AGE CAN NO MORE BE MEASURED BY VOLUME THAN BY LINEAR MEASURE . . . DEPTH ALONE EXPRESSES THE LIMITLESS/ LIMITED SPHERE THAT IS SPACE." Pevsner, *Constructivist Manifesto, Moscow 1920*.

"SPACE CANNOT BE SEEN BY THE EYE, IT IS ALL AROUND US LIKE A GLOBE STRETCHING INTO ETERNITY. SCULPTURE IS TO BE *HEARD* LIKE MUSIC." Naum Gabo, *Second Constructivist Manifesto, Berlin 1924*.

"UNTIL NOW THE THREE DIMENSIONS OF EUCLID'S GEOMETRY WERE SUFFICIENT TO THE RESTIVENESS FELT BY GREAT ARTISTS YEARNING FOR THE INFI- NITE . . . TODAY SCIENTISTS NO LONGER LIMIT THEMSELVES TO THE THREE DIMENSIONS OF EUCLID . . . A MACHINE AGE DEMANDS NON- EUCLIDEAN PAINTING . . ." Apollinaire, *Les peintres cubistes, 1913*.

The *Dadaists* of the early Twenties, however, pushed the veneration of machine-culture the furthest, ending up with a curiously pre-Existen- tialist concept of man as a machine without will or meaning.

DADA "DADA IS THE SCREAM OF BRAKES, THE METAMORPHOSIS OF MAN INTO A DYNAMO, THE BEAUTY OF WOMEN CONSIDERED AS SPARK- PLUGS, COGS AND PISTONS . . . THE LANDSCAPE TRANS- FORMED INTO ROTTEN STREETCARS AND DEAD LOCO- MOTIVES . . ." *Dada Manifesto* from *"das Hirngeschwuer" Zurich, 1919*.

Dadaist *"machinism"*, a series of biomorphic and mechanomorphic experi- ments ultimately led to Marcel Duchamp's elaborate masterpiece *"The Bride Stripped Bare by Her Bachelors"*. This fantastic juxtaposition of machine parts and mechanized biological forms became the archetypal image of much Dadaist and Surrealist painting. *Surrealism* took much of the mechanistic philosophy of the Dada movement, but changed the viewpoint from "man *as* a machine" to "man *devoured* by the machine". In Andre Breton's definition of *Surrealism*, the emphasis

SURREALISME

"SURREALISM . . . AS BEAUTIFUL AS THE CHANCE ENCOUNTER OF A SEWING MACHINE AND AN UMBRELLA ON A DISSECTING TABLE!" Andre Breton, *"Le Surrealisme au service de la revolution"*, Paris 1933.

is again on machines and technological constructs to create the hebdomadal poetics of European artists. Jazz, speed, the skyscraper is never accepted *an sich*, as a tool, a means to a technological end. Instead the magazine "TRANSITION" (Paris 1927–1938) spends its time perfecting elaborate *"Paramyths"* to gain an *a priori oral* acceptance of mechanistic muses. The American Lindbergh accepts the airplane as "transportation" and flies it to Paris; at the same time the French pilot-litterateur Antoine de Saint-Exupéry starts on a trilogy of booklength epic poems ("Night Flight", "Wind, Sand and Stars", "Flight to Arras") that elevate the smell of oil and the throbbing engine of his mail-plane to a sort of minor solar myth.

A comparison of the work of this century's greatest architects, Frank Lloyd Wright and Le Corbusier serves to illustrate the European's need for his poetical bridge into the multivalent world of technology even more: Compare say, Le Corbusier's *Ville Savoy* (1924) and his *Plan Voisin de Paris*, with Wright's *Taliesin* of the same year, or his city-planning concept of *Broadacre City*.

"THE MACHINE IS HERE TO STAY. THE ARTIST MUST USE IT AS A TOOL, LIKE HAMMER OR ADZE . . . HE MUST NOT VENERATE IT OR MAKE A POEM ABOUT IT . . ." Frank Lloyd Wright, *"Wendingen Portfolio"* Santpoort, Holland 1925.

3

"THE BEAUTY OF 'LES AUTOS, LES AVIONS, LES PAQUEBOTS' IS THE POETRY OF OUR AGE . . . THE HOUSE IS '*LE MACHINE A HABITER*'!" Le Corbusier in "*Le Corbusier: Oevre Complete de 1910–1929*" Erlenbach Verlag, Zurich.

In the *Ville Savoy* the "*machine a habiter*" has been glorified to the point where the actual human requirements of the occupants have been rigidly truncated to mold human needs into a pattern more acceptable to the machine. Many of the apparent machine-operations that went into the structure of the house are faked by hand-craftsmen.

Wright's *Taliesin* by comparison is a romantic, fully space-time developed structure, impossible to create without a highly developed technological society, using the machine as part of the everyday architectural vocabulary. The building (unlike Le Corbusier's linear-argued packing-crates on stilts) explodes all interior space into its site, placing the human being and his archetypal central hearth in a constantly shifting focus, with spatial movement possible in *all* directions.

Similarly, Le Corbusier's Paris plan presents vistas of anti-human skyscrapers raised to the stature of demi-gods, huge sterile machines-for-living that might serve Karel Capek's *Rossum's Universal Robots* (Karel Capek: "R.U.R.", Prague and New York 1933) rather than human beings. Wright's *Broadacre City*, on the other hand, is his logical biomorphic extension of *Taliesin* to city-planning.

(While an entire anectodal myth grew around Le Corbusier's *machine a habiter*, R. Buckminster Fuller in the United States built his first fully *Dymaxion house*, leading logically to his *Geodesic Domes* of today: spherical and demi-spherical shelters that are closer to true auditory space than any other structures now extant (or than their own designer realizes, for that matter!)

We have Wright then, using the crafts of the machine to build a technological bridge to poetic, acoustical space; we see Le Corbusier verbalizing his structural philosophy to erect his poetical '*Bruecke*' to North American technology.

Take the painter then. Whether it is Ryder or Sargent, Harnett and his *trompe l'oeil*, Norman Rockwell's sacharine covers for the *Saturday Evening Post*, Charles Sheeler or Salvador Dali, their preoccupation has been to paint N O U N S. To paint NOUNS, NOUN-objects, things-in-themselves, tags, identifications in other words.

4

WHEN WE IDENTIFY . . . WE DISREGARD THE IN-
HERENT DIFFERENCES, AND SO PROPER EVALUA-
TION AND FULL EXPERIENCE BECOMES IMPOSSIBLE.
Alfred Korzybski: *"SCIENCE AND SANITY: An Introduction
to Non-Aristotelian Systems and General Semantics."* 1933.

WE LIVE IN A FOUR-DIMENSIONAL SPACE-TIME
MANIFOLD WHICH, ON ALL LEVELS, CONSISTS OF
ABSOLUTELY INDIVIDUAL EVENTS, OBJECTS, SITUA-
TIONS, ABSTRACTIONS ETC., AND WE MUST CON-
CLUDE THAT STRUCTURALLY WE LIVE IN AN *IN-
DEFINITELY MANY-VALUED* OR INFINITE-VALUED
WORLD, WHERE . . . IDENTIFICATION BECOMES
IMPOSSIBLE. Alfred Korzybski, Ibid.

And to paint nouns and put them down in a linear way, like a catalogue
listing: 1), 2), 3), 4, etc. . . . and sometimes someone like Dali paints his
nouns still but disarranges and juxtaposes them like: 3), 18), 1), 657),
2); but they are still nouns, painted noun-things in a lineal or disarranged
lineal order. (The Chinese, it is interesting to note, when enumerating
or listing items, head the various paragraphs: 1), 1), 1), 1), 1), etc.,
to show the simultaneous importance of all points listed!) The forever
identifying noun-painter then, is inextricably involved with linear space
constructs. Space-time concepts have no existence for him: he will
attempt to "paint a tree". (And the only way to paint a tree is with a
stepladder and an extra large bucket of paint.)

"THE ONLY WAY TO SEE THE *'GUERNICA'* IS TO FEEL
ONESELF INTO ITS CENTER!" Picasso: *"Poemas y Decla-
raciones"*, Mexico 1945.

But the avant-garde European artist, result of a largely oral culture and
less tied to linear apron-strings, reacted on a multivalent feeling-level,
responded *haptically* and tried to avoid identifying *noun* painting.

5

PICASSO

"... Anyway an image is a thing and things cannot enter art. An art-act is feeling in action.

Picasso's painting is always exciting because Picasso paints the path of feeling. I am speaking completely literally. Picasso paints the path of feeling.
Did you ever have a teardrop run down your face?
Sometime have a teardrop run down your face and feel it run. Feel it run and then you will understand Picasso. Picasso paints a teardrop running down your face. He paints a tragic *running down* on *the face* . . . just as you would feel it. Then at the end of the running he paints the tear-drop . . . as it feels. He paints the path of the teardrop . . . He paints a path of feeling . . . He paints the path of every feeling he has at the moment he is feeling. A moment later would be too late.
It is so simple.
Picasso paints a teardrop when it is running down the face. That is all.
Of course he must paint the *when*. He paints it *when* it is running . . . all the way. He does not paint the teardrop itself until it has stopped running. Then the teardrop hangs suspended from the *when* like it feels on the face.
It is not only of Picasso that I speak. There are others . . . like Miro like Chagall like Mondrian like Brancusi and Braque and Kandinsky and Klee . . . "
Louis Danz: Personal Revolution and Picasso

Piet Mondrian's *"Broadway Boogie-Woogie"* is such a *when* painting. Probably the most interesting attempts to abolish the linear book-tradition in the arts were carried on at the German *Bauhaus* in the Twenties. The most direct and remarkable of these is contained in Moholy-Nagy's book *"MALEREI, FOTOGRAFIE UND FILM"* (Langen Verlag, Munich

6

1925). This is a large 16-page pot-pourri of typography, photographs, musical notes, symbols letterforms and brief poems, called *"DYNAMIK DER GROSSSTADT"* in which all the various visual units are to be *"heard simultaneously"* (Moholy-Nagy's italics) to form an impression of a great modern city. Frequently the type becomes so (meaningfully) distorted that I am tempted to describe it as *ONOMATOPEIC TYPO-GRAPHY*. In the May 1936 issue of *"TELEHOR"*, a Czech-slovak avant-garde magazine, Moholy-Nagy wishes it were:

". . . POSSIBLE TO CREATE CANVASSES ON THE INTERIOR SURFACES OF SPHERES, INTO WHICH SPECTATORS COULD INSERT THEIR HEADS. THUS THE TRUE NATURE OF MULTI-DIMENSIONAL, END-LESSLY SPHERICAL SPACE WOULD BE USED FULLY AND HEAD-MOVEMENTS AS WELL AS PERIPHERAL VISION WOULD COMPENSATE FOR THE *STATIC, EUCLIDEAN CHARACTER* OF THE EASEL PAINTING."

Oskar Schlemmer's stage workshop (also at the *Bauhaus*) translated the dynamics of the machine into a *"TRIADIC BALLET"*, a robot-like heavily costumed dance, reminiscent of George Antheil's *"Ballet Mechanique"* and his *"Airplane Sonata"*, attempting to:

"TURN THE DANCERS INTO PISTONS AND COG-WHEELS, TO SUBORDINATE THE INDIVIDUAL DANCER TO THE POETICS OF THE ALL-ENFOLDING MACHINE, AND TO *COMMUNICATE SIMULTANE-OUSLY AND ON ALL LEVELS* THE WILD CACOPHONY OF AUTO, SKYSCRAPER-CITY AND JAZZ. . . ." Oskar Schlemmer and L. Moholy-Nagy: *"Die Buehne im Bauhaus"* Langen Verlag, Munich 1924.

But the most direct attack against the strangle hold which the lineal book culture exerted on the arts came from the Dutch art movement *DE STIJL* and its leaders Mondrian, Theo van Doesburg and Antony Kok: Even, to turn aside from the plastic arts for the moment, Dr. C. G. Jung in his *"Randbemerkungen zur Erklaerung der Alchemie"* discusses the archetypal image of the *great worm Uroboros* and says that:

". . . IT (the worm) SHOULD REALLY BE IMAGINED AS FULLY *SPHERICAL RATHER THAN LINEAR*, ALONG THE LINES OF THE TOPOLOGIST'S *MOEBIUS-STRIP* OR *KLEIN'S BOTTLE*." (Italics mine)

THE ADMISSION OF THE ENERGY OF CHANGE INTO THE STATIC CORE OF THREE-DIMENSIONAL REALITY WAS BOUND TO RESULT IN A WHOLLY ENERGETIC WORLD OF TOTAL CHANGEABILITY. THE TRADITIONAL STATIC GROUND DEEPENED INTO THE SUBSTRATUM OF PURE ENERGIES. THE RESULT IS A WIDER AND FREER VISION OF A WORLD WITH THE STRONGER UNITY OF IRREDUCIBLE OPEN GROWTH . . . THUS, THE TRADITIONAL SENSUOUS SURFACE, SYMBOLIZING THREE-DIMENSIONAL STATIC DEPTH, APPEARS AS FLAT TO THE MODERN MIND AS THE MAGIC PICTURE OF REALITY ONCE APPEARED TO THE RATIONAL MIND. A. Dorner *"The Way Beyond Art"*, N.Y. 1945.

How much the traditional picture of a three-dimensional world has changed may be illustrated by an example which shows the similarity of the revolutions in physics and art: Some time ago the well-known physicist Hans Reichenbach used a Charles Addams cartoon from the *New Yorker* as an illustration for the behaviour of an electron according to Heisenberg's Uncertainty Principle. Here is a tree which in an unguarded moment must suddenly not have been a tree. The source of energy which enables the electron to behave like the tree in the cartoon, namely to change its identity derived from a spatial system, seems to be illustrated by Schroedinger's world of immaterial waves which explode the static point of the electron and with it the basic immutability of a spatial world. What now holds the world together is no longer the rigid framework of space represented by static material points, but the interpenetrative force of energetic waves, a force which results in self-transforming processes. When that force of transformation is pried loose—as in a so-called electron—it behaves like our unpredictable tree.

8

The whole development of modern art has moved towards just such a picture of reality. A modern composition shows in a positive way

what the cartoon with its traditional perspective reality could only show negatively as a miraculous encroachment upon the world of space and its eternal laws of motion.

THE NEW QUANTUM PHYSICS, SCHROEDINGER'S IM-MATERIAL WAVES . . . HAVE GIVEN HIM (the artist) A NEW CONCEPT OF SPACE AS A SPHERE DYNAMICALLY EXPANDING AND YET FINITE. Wolfgang Paalen 1939.

The experiments in acoustic space of the German painter-architect Frederick Kiesler, founder of the *Correalist* movement, have led to his "Endless House" (1950), an attempt completely to break down linear structuring and finite limitations.

THE SIGN FOR "WORDS" IN THE CHINESE LANGUAGE IS COMPOSED OF FOUR PARALLEL LINES IN THE UPPER PART OF THE CHARACTER TO THE RIGHT. THE SQUARE IS THE SIGN FOR "MOUTH". TOGETHER IT MEANS "TO SPEAK".

Drawing by Chas. Addams Copr. 1940 The New Yorker Magazine Inc.

9

We see then in the development of the plastic arts in Europe during the last 45 years an acceptance of technology only after it has been extensively verbalized, and evolved into a poetically acceptable mythos. The findings of modern science (Einstein, Booleia laws, Heisenberg's uncertainty principle, Non-Euclidean Geometry, Non-Aristotelian Logic, etc., etc.) have hastened this process of returning art to a *haptic* acoustical-time level it has not occupied since the introduction of the printing press into Western Europe in the fifteenth century.

. . . SOMETIME IN OUR AGE MANKIND DISCOVERED THE POSITIVE EXISTENCE OF A FOURTH DIMENSION, AND ALL OF A SUDDEN OUR MINDS CAPTURED A NEW MEANING OF THINGS, EXPRESSED IN CONTEMPORARY SCIENCE AND ART.

THE PROBLEM OF DIMENSION RETURNS TO US WITH GREAT POWER AFTER TRANSCENDING THE FROZEN TRILOGY OF "LINE, SURFACE AND VOLUME" IN WHICH IT WAS CAST EVER SINCE EUCLIDEAN TIMES. WE REALIZE NOW THAT DIMENSION, WHETHER APPARENT OR REAL, PHYSICAL OR IMAGINARY, THIRD, FOURTH OF FIFTH, REPRESENTS OUR SUPREME AMBITION TO GOVERN THE UNIVERSE IN A MULTITUDE OF DIRECTIONS.

DIMENSION UNLIKE MEASURE, IS FLEXIBLE, AND FUNDAMENTAL AND DYNAMIC.

DIMENSION, NEITHER THE THIRD NOR THE SIXTH, BUT THE nTH HUMAN POWER TO STUDY, PROJECT, AND ORGANIZE. Manifesto from Vol. I of *"Dimension"*, Dept. of Architecture and Design, Univ. of Michigan, 1955.

It must be remembered, however, that this poetic bridge-building of Europe's verbal tradition (as well as American needs for technological bridges towards apperception of European art-values, scarcely alluded to in this essay) are temporary expedients only.

With the spread of modern mass-communication media: TV, radio, picture magazine, movie, etc., a closer and more direct oral channel is opening for all cultures.

Victor J. Papanek

10

ORAL TO WRITTEN:

Some implications of the Anglo-Saxon Transition

The early English poets made a relatively fast adjustment to the Latin culture of the Church and to vernacular literacy: Irish and Roman missionaries to England in the sixth century; a century later, Cædmon (or someone else by the same name) singing Christian epics in English. From the first, the native tradition was under pressure to conform to traditional classical and Christian models, but for many centuries it never entirely lost its oral characteristics, and indeed perhaps never has lost them, though they were obscured alomst to extinction during the Norman period and again in the eighteenth century. After the Normans, the fourteenth-century alliterative revival; after the triumph of neo-classicism, Coleridge's stress-meter for *Christabel,* the rehabilitation of native (non-syllabic) meters, and, very lately, a response to electronic techniques which led a critic of Dylan Thomas' recorded poetry to say, "Good as it is, his poetry on the printed page is dull in comparison".

The change from an oral culture of traditional singers to a book culture of readers-aloud was perhaps made smoother by the production of illustrated codices, and at the same time complicated by the bookish suppression of the musical bases of oral poetry. Thus in the richly decorated Gospel books of the Age of Bede or the sensitive linear illustrations of the tenth and eleventh centuries, the eye of a reader struggling toward fluent literacy might be distracted and delighted by pictures. This is the reverse of the present situation, in which a generation increasingly unlettered takes its literature from films, television, or bathetically, from

11

picture books of Homer, Shakespeare, Scott, and even—sweet revengeful whirligig of time!—*Beowulf*. But books of poetry were copied out, whether from dictation or composition, as page-blocks of prose, thus obliterating even an editorial suggestion of the verse's aboriginal musical structure. A visual culture would object to its poetry being printed as the Anglo-Saxon scribe might have written it, naked: *The children call and I thy shepherd pipe and sweet is every sound sweeter thy voice but every sound is sweet myriads of rivulets hurrying thro the lawn the moan of doves in immemorial elms*. . . . If we did find our verse printed so, we should turn quickly into slow-working lip-movers again. That is after all how we began as children, and acoustic reading was a feature of the medieval literary process. Why did the monks in their cloisters have carrells for study? "For the same reason that the reading-room of the British Museum is not divided into sound-proof compartments. The habit of silent reading has made such an arrangement unnecessary; but fill the reading-room with medieval readers and the buzz of whispering and muttering would be intolerable." (H. J. Chaytor, *From Script to Print*, 19.) As skilled silent readers we do not expect even a lyric poem to exist in audible musical form, but the earliest English verse was accompanied singing. What the deprivation of the music meant to an Anglo-Saxon we can partly imagine by attempting to strip from our experience of some familiar rhythmic reading the admixtures of music in it. If one wished to read aloud St. Luke ii: 9 in such a way as to emphasize the angels' democracy in appearing to mere shepherds with their great message, he would need to violate, some would say, the speech-rhythms of the King James Version.

If he is musical, however, what may truly disturb him is that he will need to violate his Handel-given birthright to remember these phrases against the musical background of a familiar epic recitative. Handel so set the text as to stress, at the beginning and middle of certain measures, the important words LO, ANgel, LORD, GLOry, and THEY, while the secondary stressed forms upON and aBOUT are prominent enough to obscure the two following objective pronouns.

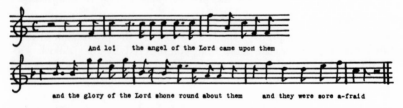

And lo! the angel of the Lord came upon them

and the glory of the Lord shone round about them   and they were sore a-fraid

The angel of the Lord came upon THEM [even them]
And the glory of the Lord shone round about THEM [not,
    for instance, about the rulers of the country]

Handel's stresses, for anyone who has heard them regularly from childhood, are formulaic and dictatorial; words and music are one experience, but in a literary (as opposed to an oral) culture, it is a comparatively rare experience. For the Anglo-Saxons of the early transition period it was common. Parchment was precious, a page-centered-verse arrangement was lacking, and the rhythms of verse appeared not only without their music but also in many cases without even the most rudimentary marks of rhythmical or rhetorical punctuation.

"It is Lawes to whom we owe *Comus*," Professor Hughes pointed out; but there are those who can read Milton's libretto silently or aloud without an aching sense of musical loss. On the other hand, Tate's relatively inferior libretto for *Dido and Aeneas* equally fails to suggest to the eye the rich score with which Purcell exalts the text. What if both libretti had outlived the seventeenth century only in manuscripts several times recopied and perhaps with a sheet or two missing? So far as Old English verse was musical, we have lost it; we possess by chance and for the most part without duplication of manuscript versions only the damaged libretti of a few early musical compositions; the poetry as a total acoustic experience we have not got.

Old English verse antedates not only sound-recording equipment but even manuscript transcription of secular music in England. We do not know to what mode a singer tuned his harp, much less how he played it, and we should probably not mourn our ignorance too sentimentally: the fullest musical transcripts, if we had them, would still be a critical distance from the real thing. RCA-Victor has released posthumously Toscanini's version of *Aïda,* an invaluable record historically but not a real performance of the opera. It is rather a sound-studio (read *scriptorium*) or symphonic (read *literary*) performance.

MS. Cotton Vitellius A.XV	RCA Victor LM 6132
Beowulf	Aïda

More to the point would be the questions that arise from the Old English static transcription of oral verse in manuscript. Bede does not tell how Cædmon's Christian epics were recorded, if they were recorded at all from his lips. "So Cædmon stored in his memory all that he learned, and after meditation rendered it in such sweet melody that his delightful verse made his teachers in turn his audience." His audience; not his scribes. Still, one presumes that in the earlier vernacular period the unlettered singers must have performed their songs for copying by a scribe. What such a process might involve by way of textual difficulties is suggested by A. B. Lord (*Serbocroatian Heroic Songs*, 7–8), who tells how the first texts in the Milman Parry collection were taken down from dictation in Yugoslavia in 1933. There the singer was at an initial disadvantage, lacking both his audience and his musical instrument, the gusle, without which he was at `a loss rhythmically. Later, because a real audience was missing, he tended to become bored and shorten his song; and since he was unused to slow composition, he tended to run ahead of the scribe-collector, who was forced to help the singer along, encouraging him but trying not to help formulate the verse himself. How closely, then, did a dictated Old English narrative represent a typical oral performance, and how much, in the surviving poems, of the stumbling obscurity, the enigmatic foreshortenings of action, the inorganic expansion of commonplace material, can be attributed to an uneasy collaboration of singer and scribe?

The experiences of Parry and Lord in Yugoslavia suggest yet another difficulty; singers who were literate would sometimes write down their own songs. If the Old English singer were also a scribe, how much (putting aside the fact that most of the surviving manuscripts were recopied perhaps for centuries after their original composition) would his own writing activity affect the transmission of his own verse? Writing of textual problems in a later period, E. T. Donaldson observes (50 *Modern Philology* 272), "In the back of some of our minds there is a clear distinction between scribes and poets, as if a scribe were a copying animal and a poet a creative one. But actually the terms only describe different functions of the single animal man. In so far as a poet copies his own work, he is a scribe and heir to the errors that beset scribality." In Anglo-Saxon England there was some mechanical and relatively accurate copying and much aimless and inaccurate copying; was there also such a thing as creative copying?

As literate authors learned to assimilate oral materials to pen-and-parchment composition, and since cultural life and centres of writing were controlled so largely by the Church, it was inevitable that the oral transmission of pagan verse would die out, or at best leave few records of an increasingly precarious existence. Meanwhile the invasion of bookish culture into an oral tradition proceeded. Amid the overwhelming anonymity of the period, Cynewulf was the only poet who troubled to record his name, not from motives of a new literary vanity, but against the Day of Judgement: "I beg every man of human kind who recites this poem *to remember my name* and pray. . . ." His poetry, however, is literary in the modern sense, in the vernacular but responsive to Latin models; he was a book-cultured man, or as Kenneth Sisam writes, "a man of letters, the first in English whose name and works are known".

Sometimes Greek and Latin culture show up rather grotesquely in the

14

old poetic meters, as, for example, in a macaronic exercise that praises Aldhelm:

Þ us me gesette *sanctus et iustus*
beorn boca gleaw, *bonus auctor,*
Ealdelm, æ þ ele sceop, *etiam fuit*
ipselos [= ὑψηλός] on æðele Angolsexna,
byscop on Bretene.

But occasionally the best traditions of the old verse and a delight in literacy fuse, as in the well-known joking riddle about a book-worm, or in the shout of triumph that concludes *Brunanburh*: "Never yet in this island was a greater slaughter of an army by the sword's edge, as books and ancient scholars tell us. . . ." That, in an oral culture, would have been an extraordinary statement for a battle-bard to make. But it is not so extraordinary as the symbol of accomplished revolution which appears in the *Gloria patri* below.

Patri et filio et spiritui sancto.
Þu eart frofra fæder and feorhhyrde,
lifes latteow, leohtes wealdend,
asyndrod from synnum, swa ðin sunu maere
þurh clæne gecynd, cyning ofer ealle,
beald gebletsod, BOCA LAREOW,
heah higefrofer and halig gast.

It unites in traditional alliterative and formulaic style a number of kennings for "God" (Father of Consolations, Life-Protector, Guide of Life, Master of Light . . .) among which towards the climax comes *boca laerow*, "Master of Books". It is the implication of this single expression that the oral responsibility of the scop has vanished. The maker had become writer, and he would remain essentially voiceless to the large public until the technological revolution of our own time.

Not that the literary virtue of a recorded poet-reader today is necessarily less ambiguous than that of a poet-scribe a thousand years ago; not every contemporary master of books is as skilled before the microphone as Dylan Thomas or James Joyce.

Coventry Patmore in *English Metrical Law*: "*Perfect* readers of high poetry are as rare as fine singers and good composers, for the sufficient reason, that they *are* fine singers and good composers, though they may not suspect it in an age of unnatural divorce of sound and sense."

J. B. Bessinger

15

THIRD PROGRAM IN THE HUMAN AGE

Stephen Spender once suggested that the reason there is no more avant-garde experiment in literature is that this role has been assumed by the new media of expression.

Retrospectively, most verbal experiment since the Romantics has taken the form of transferring to verbal manifestations on the page devices and modalities from elsewhere. Wordsworth and his followers had a conscious program of evoking and fixing mental states via the picturesque' devices of landscape art. They were well aware of the book as their rival and antagonist in this adventure.

Rimbaud and Mallarmé were the first to adopt the modalities of the newspaper and illustrated magazines to the organization of poetic effects. They cocked their snoots at all literature: 'Littérature, c'est la banalité.' Meanwhile the novel in the hands of Scott and Dickens built up a massive anticipation of the movie form of narrative and characterization. So that if Ulysses in 1922 spelled the transcendance and also the end of the novel, the movie did the same tale repeat in the same decade.
But the movie type of impressionism also gave the novel new life in the work of Hemingway and Dos Passos. Verbal art acquired new dimensions in going to school to cinema.

Henry James' style was transformed in the 90's by his new habit of dictation. The alchemy of the media between themselves and upon their audiences is a totally unexplored subject. But why should it be doubted that radio and TV will transform prose and verse styles? Or how could anybody, in view of the history of such transformations, wish that they would cease to affect language and expression? The difference between the artist and the organization man in these matters would seem to be that the artist senses at once the creative possibilities in new media even when they are alien to his own medium, whereas the bureaucrat of arts and letters moans and bristles whenever his museum of exhibits is threatened by invasion or desertion. The artist is the historian of the future because he uses the unnoticed possibilities of the present.

Wyndham Lewis is perhaps the first creative writer to have taken over the new media *en bloc* as modes of artistic and social control. (Joyce and Eliot have done so on a smaller scale.) In *Apes of God,* Pierpont's 'broadcasting' is central to the esthetic effect of that work. In *The Childermass,* movie dissolve and montage are the very mode of presentation of scene and character. The effect of daily technological and social change in society at large is encoded in the Marx-brother sequences between the characters Pullman and Satters:

> Satters is a thing of the past. The time-and-class-scales in which they hang in reciprocal action are oscillating violently, as they rush up and down through neighbouring dimensions they sight each other only very imperfectly. . . . Satters as Keystone giant receives the crack exactly in the right spot, he sags forward in obedient overthrow, true to type. . . .

As they move toward the Magnetic City, Pullman and Satters are caught in a brief but violent storm:

> I'm not surprised. The Bailiff will be up quite soon now. . . . They say the Bailiff sends a storm every morning to clear the atmosphere so that he can be comfortable.

The storm, of course, is concocted by news releases and headlines, and the Bailiff Lord of the Magnetic City is a press lord:

> The officials never cease to mop their brows. The Bailiff alone appears cool. . . . Directed to the adjusting of the niceties of salvation. this administrative unit yet displays the untidiness and fatigue of a secular community. An hysteria is noticed to sweep over it whenever its routine is disturbed. . . .
>
> After some minutes the Bailiff reappears . . . the lymph of a bottomless obtuseness appears to invade his beaked heavy and shining mask. . . . In his hands he slowly revolves the pivetta used by the atellan actors to mimic the voices of the mimes of classical tragedy.

The ensuing news barrage occurs simultaneously in sight and sound:

> Snorting *Battery.* Unseen scale-snob swells snorting in the darkness and is silenced in arithmetic. . . . 'It's getting worse', he says. 'I shouldn't

17

stare too much if I were you. It's a great strain on the eyes. . . . It's five thousand years away.'

The high point of *The Childermass* occurs when the Bailiff assumes the costume of a Limerick playboy and canters and steins his way through several pages of mock Finneganese. These antics he refers to as his own press lord operations: '. . . having explained to you the principle of my prattle, I hope you understood it. Nexpleece!'

In *Monstre Gai* and *Malign Fiesta*, which make up *The Human Age*, the Bailiff resumes his protean Press Lord role, but in the loftier and more austere dimensions of Third City he appears as a shabby public relations gent. He's a *Washington Confidential* sort. Lewis now refers to the Magnetic City as 'Third City' and makes it explicit that this particular level of the Dantesque comedy is the BBC's Third Program:

All are vegetarians, perforce. There is no meat to be had. But unless you are inveterately carnivorous, you will soon forget that. . . . No, there is no meat, no women, no alcohol, no telephones. . . . There is a good deal of homosexuality. And, as I have said, the air is like champagne! You are in a degenerate, chaotic outpost of Heaven. The ostensible ruler, the Padishah, is a supernatural being of great charm, but devoid of the slightest trace of gumption. . . . There is no man in the city who has been here beyond the Tudors. . . . The entire show is one great farce. It is far sillier even than life on earth—for at least that was centred upon the mechanical purpose of perpetuating the species. Someone or something seemed crazily set upon that happening. There is no *entetement* of that kind here. Provided with money by the State, they exist in suspended animation, sexless, vegetarian, and dry, permanently about forty-six. If you can see any sense in it, I can't.

It is, however, after leaving Third City for Matapolis that Lewis provides his most subtle and extensive correlations between Hell and the technology of our new media. With the help of modern scientific medicine he re-edits and refurnishes the various levels of Dante's *Inferno* in a startling way. The Devils appear as film stars perturbed by the ease with which their supernatural dimensions are mimicked by modern publicity devices. It's this power of the new media which fosters a new humanist movement in Hell. The Devil, Pullman sees as:

Now arranging for the contamination of the angel nature—for the destruction of something which had endured since the beginning of time. He was going to mix it up with the pettiness and corruption of mankind. He had built for it, in Angeltown, a sort of comic Hollywood. Now he was forcing upon it woman—with all her sexishness, her nursery-mind, her vulgarity.

Marshall McLuhan

THE SEMANTICS OF MONEY-USES

Because of the exchange use of money under our market organization of economic life we are apt to think of money in too narrow terms. No object is money *per se,* and any object in an appropriate field can function as money. In truth, money is a system of symbols similar to language, writing, or weights and measures. These differ from one another mainly in the purpose served, the actual symbols employed, and the degree to which they display a single unified purpose.

Pseudo-philosophies of money
Money is an incompletely unified system, a search for its single purpose a blind alley. This accounts for the many unavailing attempts at determining the 'nature and essence' of money. We must be content with listing the purposes to which the quantifiable objects actually called money are put. This is achieved by pointing to the situation in which we operate those objects and with what effect. We will find them called money, when used in any one of the following ways: for payment; as a standard; as a means of indirect exchange. The human situation is, of course, given independently of the notion of money, just as the handling of the objects is described in operational terms independently of that notion. Payment occurs in a situation of obligation and a handing over of the objects has the effect of wiping out the obligation. Money used as a standard is a quantitative tag attached to units of goods of different kinds, either for the purpose of barter with the effect that, by adding up the numerals, we can readily equalize the two sides in the

exchange, or for budgeting and balancing stores of different staples, thus producing staple finance. Finally, there is the exchange use of such objects, that is, acquiring them in order to acquire other objects through a further act of exchange. The objects employed in direct exchange thereby gain the character of money. They become symbols through their participation in a definite human situation.

A few side-lines are here avoided. First: The distinction between tokens and what they 'represent' is ignored. Either function as money objects and form part of the symbolic system. No difference is therefore made between barley money, gold money, paper money. To confuse the basic problem of money with that of token money is a source of frequent misunderstandings. Tokens as such are no novelty—fiction and abstraction belong to the original endowment of man. In Herodotus' well-known story of compulsory temple prostitution in Babylonia, he records this operational detail: 'The silver coin may be of any size; it cannot be refused for that is forbidden by the law, since, once thrown, it is sacred.' Nor are mere tokens unknown in the primitive societies of our ethnographers. Some peoples of the Congo employ 'simply as a token' straw mats or grass cloth originally of square shape, but eventually reduced to a tangle of hay, 'practically of no value at all'. Strips of blue cloth of standard width that had become in time useless rags were current as token money in parts of the Western Sudan. However, since paper money came to the fore, scholars felt induced to focus on the tokens instead of on the massive physical objects themselves. This modernizing fashion carried the day. The latest outstanding work of an ethnographer, Mrs. Quiggin, takes the token to be the true money and accordingly dubs the actual money objects that it describes exhaustively, 'money substitues'. Historians of antiquity have proved hardly less susceptible to modernizing on the matter of money. Since third millennium Babylonia possessed no paper money, the metals were regarded by historians as the orthodox money material. Actually, all payments were made in barley. Bruno Meissner, the Assyriologist, put this in the terms 'Money was primarily replaced by grain.' His colleague Lutz thought that the scarcity of silver 'necessitated the use of a substitute. Thus grain often took the place of metals.' Throughout, token money ranks as true money, since it's the most abstract and the least useful; next comes gold and silver, as substitutes; in their absence, even grain will do. This is a consistent reversal of the sequence in which the physical money objects are primary empirical evidence. Yet the existence of tokens should cause no complications; it is a matter of course in a monetary system. If paper money viewed as a token, 'symbolizes' coins, then in our terms it symbolizes that which is already a symbol, namely money. Symbols do not merely 'represent' something. They are material, oral, visual, or purely imaginary signs that form part of the definite situation in which they participate; thus they acquire meaning.

Second: A similar disregard of the semantics of economic theory is forced upon us in the choice of terms when referring to the various money uses. Payment, standard, and means of exchange are distinctions originally developed by classical economists. Hence the understandable belief of some anthropologists that their application to primitive money implies an economistic bias. The reverse would be truer. Actually, modern economics does not rely for its monetary theories on such distinctions at all. Archaic society, on the other hand, shows an institutional setting where the use of quantifiable objects typically occurs in precisely those three ways.

All-purpose and special-purpose money
From a formal angle, modern money, in contrast to primitive money, offers a striking resemblance to both language and writing. They all possess a uniform grammar. All three are organized in an elaborate code of rules concerning the correct way of employing the symbols—and general rules applicable to all the symbols. Archaic society knows not 'all-purpose' money. Various money-uses may be supplied here by different money objects. Consequently, there is no grammar with which all money-uses must comply. No one kind of object deserves the distinctive name of money; rather the term applies to a small group of objects, each of which may serve as money in a different way. While in modern society the money employed as a means of exchange is endowed with the capacity of performing all the other functions as well, in early society the position is rather the reverse. One encounters slaves or horses or cattle used as a standard when judging of prestige conveying wealth, or anyway of large amounts, while cowrie shells are solely employed for small amounts. (Eventually, the unit slave or horse may stand for a conventional value representing a mere unit of account, real slaves and horses being actually sold at varying prices.) We might also find that while real slaves are a means of payment of tribute to a foreign overlord, cowrie shells function as a domestic means of payment or even as a medium of exchange. This may not exclude the use of precious metals for hoarding wealth, while such metals may not otherwise serve as money except perhaps as a standard, and in exchange for imports. Where the market habit is fairly wide-spread money might moreover serve as a means of exchange to which end several trade goods might be in use, which otherwise are not employed as money at all. Numerous combinations of these variants occur. No *one* rule is universally valid, except for the very general but no less significant rule that money-uses are distributed between a multiplicity of different objects.

21

No such fragmentation in the use of sounds is known in any language. In speech all articulate oral sounds, in script all letters of the alphabet are eligible for use in all types of words, while archaic money in extreme cases employs one kind of object as means of payment, another as a standard of value, a third for storing wealth, and a fourth for exchange purposes—like a language where verbs consisted of one group of letters, nouns of another, adjectives of a third, and adverbs of yet a fourth.

Moreover, in primitive society exchange is not the fundamental money-use. If any one be more 'basic' than another it is rather the use for payment or standard. These are common even where the exchange use of money is not practised. Accordingly, while in modern society the unification of the various uses of money happened on the basis of its exchange-use, in early communities we find the different money-uses institutionalized separately of one another. In so far as there is interdependence between them, we find use for payment, or as a standard, or for storing of wealth, having precedence over use for exchange.

Thus 19th century money, employing exchange symbols for various other uses, appears as an almost complete parallel to language and writing with its all-purpose sounds and signs. But to some extent the analogy holds also for primitive and archaic money, which differs from its modern counterpart only in the lesser degree to which the systems are unified. However, since the second quarter of the 20th century, starting with Nazi Germany, 'modern' money begins to show a definite tendency towards a reverting to disunification. Half a dozen 'Marks' were current under Hitler and each of them restricted to some special purpose or other.

Exchange-money

'Money is a means of exchange.' This presumption belongs among the most powerful in the field of modern thought. Its authority may be gauged by the axiomatic manner in which it was formulated to cover the whole course of human history and even extended by anthropologists to primitive society. It is forcefully expressed in the following quotation: 'In any economic system, however primitive, an article can only be regarded as true money', Prof. Raymond Firth declares, 'when it acts as a definite and common medium of exchange, as a convenient stepping stone in obtaining one type of goods for another. However, in so doing, it serves as a measure of value, allowing the worth of all other articles to be expressed in terms of itself. Again, it is a standard of value, with reference to past or future payments, while as a store of value it allows wealth to be condensed and held in reserve.' (Art. 'Currency, primitive' in *Encyclopedia Britannica*, 14th ed.)

According to this still current view, the exchange-use to which money can be put is its essential criterion, not only in modern, but also in primitive society. Even under primitive conditions the various money-uses are asserted to be inseparable. Only quantifiable objects serving as means of exchange can, therefore, be regarded as money. Their functioning as means of payment, as standard of value, or as means of hoarding wealth, is not decisive for their character as money, unless it implies their use as media of exchange. For it is this use which logically unifies the system, since it allows a consistent linking up of the various functions of money. Without it there can not be true money.

Such a modernising approach to the problem, we submit, is largely responsible for the obscurity in which the characteristics of primitive money still abide.

The payment-use of money

Payment is the discharge of an obligation through the handing over of quantifiable objects, which then function as money. The connectedness of payment with money and of obligations with economic transactions appears to the modern-mind self-evident. Yet the quantification which we associate with payment operated already at a time when the obligations discharged were quite unconnected with economic transactions.

The story starts with the propinquity of payment and punishment on the one hand, obligation and guilt on the other. However, no unilineal development should be inferred. Rather, obligations may have origins different from guilt and crime, such as wooing and marriage; punishment may spring from other than sacral sources, such as prestige and precedence; eventual payment, then, with its quantitative connotation, may include operational elements not entailed in punishment as such.

It is only broadly true that civil law followed on penal law, penal law on socral law. Payment was due alike from the guilty, the defiled, the impure, the weak and the lowly; it was owed to the gods and their priests, the honoured, the pure and the strong. Punishment, accordingly, aimed at diminution in power, sanctity, prestige, status or wealth of the payer, not stopping at his physical destruction.

Pre-legal obligations mostly spring from custom and give rise to an offence only in case of default. Even so the restoring of the balance need not involve payment. Obligations are, as a rule, specific, and their fulfilment is a qualitative affair, thus lacking an essential of payment—its quantitative character. Infringement of sacral and social obligations, whether towards god, tribe, kin, totem, village, age-group, caste or guild, is repaired not through payment but by action of the right *quality*. Wooing, marrying, avoiding, dancing, singing, dressing, feasting, lamenting, lacerating, or even killing oneself may occur in discharge of an obligation, but they are not for that reason payments.

The specific characteristic in the payment-use of money is quantification.

Punishment approximates payment when the process of riddance of guilt is numerable, as when lashes of the whip, turns of the praying mill, or days of fasting dispose of the offence. But though it has now become an 'obligation to pay', the offence is atoned for not by depriving one's self of quantifiable objects, but primarily by a loss of personal qualitative values, or sacral and social status.

The payment-use of money links up with the economy when the units discharged by the person under obligation happen to be physical objects such as sacrificial animals, slaves, ornamental shells, or measures of food stuffs. The obligations may still be predominantly non-transactional, such as paying a fine, composition, tax, tribute, making gifts and counter-gifts, honouring the gods, ancestors or the dead. However, there is now a significant difference. For the payee does gain what the payer loses—the effect of the operation fits the legal concept of payment.

The ultimate intent of the obligation to pay may still be the diminution in power and status of the payer. In archaic society an exorbitant fine did not only bankrupt but politically undo the victim. For a long time power and status in this way retained their precedence over economic possessions as such. The political and social importance of accumulated wealth under these conditions lay in the rich man's capacity of making a big payment without undermining his status. (This is the condition of affairs in archaic democracies where political confiscation takes the form of exorbitant fines.) Treasure gains great political importance, as witness Thucydides' memorable passages in the Archeology. Wealth is here directly transmuted into power. It is a self-maintaining institution. Because the rich man is powerful and honoured he receives payments: gifts and dues are showered upon him without his having to use power to torture and kill. Yet his wealth, used as a fund for gifts, would procure him a sufficiency of power to do so.

Once money as a means of exchange is established in society, the practice of payment spreads far and wide. For with the introduction of markets as the physical locus of exchange a new type of obligation comes into prominence as the legal residue of transactions. Payment appears as the counter-part of some material advantage gained in the transaction. Formerly a man was made to pay taxes, rent, fines or blood-money. Now he pays for the goods he bought. Money is now means of payment *because* it is means of exchange. The notion of an independent origin of payment fades and the millennia in which it sprang not from economic transactions, but directly from religious, social or political obligations, are forgotten.

Hoarding or storage-use of money

A subordinate money-use—storing of wealth—has its origin largely in the need for payments. Payment isn't primarily an economic phenomenon. Neither is wealth. In early society it consisted largely of treasure which is again rather a social than a subsistence category. The subsistence connotation of wealth (as of payment) derives from the frequency with which wealth is accumulated in the form of cattle, slaves, and non-perishable goods of common consumption. Both that which feeds the store of wealth and that which is disbursed from it gains then a subsistence significance. Only within limits, however, since payments are still made as a rule for non-transactional reasons. This is true both of the rich who own the store of wealth, and the subjects who fill the store by their payments. He who owns wealth is thereby enabled to pay fines, composition, taxes, etc. for sacral, political and social ends. The payments which he receives from his subjects, high or low, are paid to him as taxes, rents, gifts, etc., not for transactional but for social and political reasons ranging from pure gratitude for protection or admiration of superior endowment, to stark fear of enslavement and death.

This again, is not to deny that once exchange-money is present money will readily lend itself as a store of wealth. But, as in the case of payment, the condition is the previous establishment of quantifiable objects as media of exchange.

Use of money as a standard
Money as a standard of value seems more closely linked with the exchange-use of money than is either payment or hoarding. For barter and storage of staples are the two very different sources from which the need for a standard springs. At first sight the two have little in common. The first is akin to transaction, the other to administration and disposal. Yet neither can be effectively carried out in the absence of some standard. For how otherwise than with the help of computation could, for instance, a piece of land be bartered against an assortment consisting of a chariot, horse-harness, asses, ass-harness, oxen, oil, clothes and other minor items? In the absence of a means of exchange the account in a well-known case of barter in ancient Babylonia shaped up like this. The land was valued at 816 shekels of silver, while the articles given in exchange were valued in shekels of silver as follows: chariot 100, 6 horse-harnesses 300, an ass 130, ass-harness 50, and ox 30, the rest were distributed over the smaller items.

The same principle applied, in the absence of exchange, to the administration of vast palace and temple stores (staple finance). Their keeper handled subsistence goods under conditions which from more than one angle required a gauging of the relative importance of these goods. Hence the famed rule of accountancy of 'one unit of silver = one unit of barley' on the stele of Manistusu as well as at the head of the Laws of Eshnunna.

Research data reveal that the exchange-use of money cannot have given rise to the other money uses. On the contrary, the payment, storage and accountancy uses of money had their separate origins and were institutionalized independently of one another.

Élite circulation and staple finance

It seems almost self-contradictory to expect that one could pay with money with which one can not buy. Yet that precisely is implied in the assertion that money was not used as a medium of exchange and still was used as a means of payment.

Two institutions of early society offer a partial explanation: treasure and staple finance.

Treasure, as we saw, should be distinguished from other forms of stored wealth. The difference lies mainly in its relation to subsistence. In the proper sense of the term, treasure is formed of prestige goods, including 'valuables' and ceremonial objects, the mere possession of which endows the holder with social weight, power and influence. It is, then, a peculiarity of treasure that both the giving and the receiving enhances prestige; it largely circulates for the sake of the turnover, which is its proper use. Even when food is 'treasured' it is liable to pass backwards and forwards between the parties, however absurd this might appear from the subsistence point of view. But food rarely functions as treasure, for interesting food, like slaughtered pigs, does not keep, and that which keeps, such as barley or oil, is not exciting. The precious metals, on the other hand, which are almost universally valued as treasure, can not readily be exchanged for subsistence, since apart from exceptionally auriferous regions such as the Gold Coast or Lydia, display of gold by the common people is opprobrious.

Nevertheless, treasure, like other sources of power, may be of great economic importance, since gods, kings and chiefs can be made to put the services of their dependents at the disposal of the giver, thus indirectly securing for him food, raw materials and labour services, on a large scale. Ultimately, this power of indirect disposal, which may comprise the important power of taxation, arises, of course, from the enhanced influence exerted by the recipient of treasure over his tribe or people.

All this holds good, whether the treasure consists of quantifiable units or not. If it does, the handling of treasure may give rise to something in the nature of finance. In archaic Greece, for instance, he who owned treasure employed it to gain the favour of gods and chiefs or other politically influential agents, by forming the gold and silver into conventionally acceptable gifts, such as tripods, or bowls. But this did

26

not make tripods into money, for only by an artificial construction could such an honorific gift-use be subsumed under either payment or exchange. Transactions of treasure finance were restricted to the narrow circle of the gods and chiefs. While some things could be paid for with treasure, very many more could not be bought with it.

Storage of wealth as an institution of the subsistence economy starts from the collecting and stacking of *staples*. While treasure and treasure finance does not as a rule belong to the subsistence economy, the storing of staples represents an accumulation of subsistence goods involving, as a rule, their use as a means of payment. For once staples are stored on a large scale by temple, palace or manor, this must be accompanied by such a use. Thus treasure-finance is replaced by staple-finance.
Most archaic societies possess an organization of staple-finance of some kind or other. It was in the framework of the planned transfer and investment of staples stored on a gigantic scale that the accounting devices were first developed which characterized the redistributive economies of the ancient empires over long periods of time. For only well after the introduction of coined money in Greece some six centuries before our era, did money-finance begin to supersede staple-finance in these empires, especially in the Roman Republic. Nevertheless, even later, Ptolemaic Egypt continued in the traditions of staple-finance, which it raised to unparalleled levels of efficiency.

Redistribution as a form of integration often involves under primitive conditions the storage of goods at a centre, whence they are distributed and fall out of circulation. Goods passed on as payment to the centre are passed out from there and are consumed. They provide subsistence for army, bureaucracy and labour force, whether paid out in wages, in soldiers' pay or in other forms. The personnel of the temples consumes a large part of the payments made to the temple in kind. The raw materials are required for the equipment of the army, for public works and government exports; wool and cloth are exported too; barley, oil, wine, dates, garlic, and so on, are distributed and consumed. Thus the means of payment are destroyed. Maybe some of them are eventually bartered privately by their recipients. To that extent a 'secondary circulation' is started which might even become the mainspring of local markets without disrupting the redistributive economy. Actually, no evidence of the existence of such markets has yet turned up.
The relevance of treasure and staple to the question of money-uses is therefore that they explain the functioning of the various money-uses in the absence of the market system.

Treasure goods which happen to be quantifiable may be used for payment. Yet such élite goods are not normally exchanged and cannot be used for purchase except in the sacral and foreign policy sphere. The much larger sector of payments concerns, of course, subsistence goods. Such objects, when used for the discharge of obligations, i.e., for payment, are stored at the centre whence they revert through redistributive payment and are consumed.

Treasure and staples, between them, offer therefore broadly the answer to the institutional problem set by the conditions of early society, where means of payment may be independent of the exchange use of money. The absence of money as a means of exchange in the irrigational empires helped to develop a kind of banking enterprise—actually large estate managements practicing staple finance—in order to facilitate transfer and clearing in kind. It might be added that similar methods were employed by the administrations of the larger temples. Thus clearing, book-transfer and non-transferable checks were first developed, not as expedients in a money economy, but on the contrary, as administrative devices designed to make barter more effective and therefore the developing of market methods unnecessary.

Babylonia and Dahomey
In regard to its monetary organization, Hammurabi's Babylonia, in spite of its complex economic administration and elaborate operational practices, was typically 'primitive', for the principle of differentiation of money-objects was firmly established. With many important reservations as to detail, the following broad generalization can be made: rents, wages and taxes were paid in barley, while the standard of value was universally silver. The total system was governed by the rule of accountancy, unshakably grounded on the equation '1 *shekel* of silver = 1 *gur* of barley'. In case of a permanent improvement in the average yield of the land (as would be caused by large scale irrigational works), the barley content of the *gur* was raised by solemn proclamation. The general use of silver as money of account facilitated barter enormously; the equally general employment of barley as a means of domestic payment made the storage system possible on which the redistributive economy of the country rested.
It appears that all the important staples functioned to some extent as means of exchange, none of them being permitted to attain the status of 'money' (as opposed to goods). This may also be put in the following terms: an elaborate system of barter was practised which was based on the function of silver as money of account; the use of barley as a means of payment; and the simultaneous employment of a number of staples such as oil, wool, dates, bricks, etc. as means of exchange. Amongst the latter should be counted barley and silver, care being taken to prevent these or any other staple developing into a 'preferred means of exchange'.

28

or, as we should say, money. These safeguards included the avoidance of coined money, the hoarding of precious metals in palace and temple treasury, and, more effective than all, strict legal provisions as to the documentation of transactions. The outstanding provision appears to have been the restriction of formal 'sale-purchase' transactions to *specific* goods such as a plot of land, a house, heads of cattle, individual slaves, a boat,—all of them specimens which might be designated by a name. In regard to staples or fungible goods, such as barley, oil, wool, or dates, no documentation of exchange against each other is in evidence during the millennia of cuneiform civilization.

On a very much smaller scale the 18th century Negro kingdom of Dahomey shows monetary conditions not so dissimilar to those of Babylonia. Cowries were used as domestic currency in all four uses, but as a standard of value they were supplemented by slaves which served as money of account for larger amounts. Accordingly, the wealth of rich persons, the customs payments of foreign ships to the king, tribute to foreign sovereigns, were reckoned (but only in this last instance, paid) in slaves. These did not, however, here serve as a means of exchange, as in some Haussa regions. In this latter use cowrie was supplemented by gold dust, which was especially employed in ports of trade and other foreign contacts. As to storage of wealth, not only cowrie but also slaves were used. It's reminiscent of Babylonia that the rule of accountancy governing the system involved equation between slaves and cowrie, which it seems, was a matter of public proclamation; so was the export price of slaves, which was reckoned in ounces of gold dust.

Karl Polanyi

BROWNSON ON COMMON LAW AND THE ORAL TRADITION

For three centuries scholars have themselves been so much a part of the written tradition that they have ignored what survived of the pre-literate past. Even when survivals of that past clashed with literate instruments of our civilization, the explanations that were proffered were in terms of evolution, growth, progress toward some ideal of civilization envisioned as the acme of an expressly literate society. It is this persistence within himself of literate traits and habits that is the most exasperating hindrance for the observer of changing society today. Trained in one of the scholarly—that is, literate—disciplines, he observes, studies, writes, and revises in the language of his speciality, prevented by his own expertness in his field from making the ironically termed *fresh* approach. An escape from this self-confinement is "to jump fields" to find in your colleague's area something he has seen so often in its literate category that your curiosity can only amuse him. Common law is, in fact, so common for the legal historian that he cannot see its role in the great historic change from the oral to the written tradition. Except for Orestes Brownson, an outsider of a century ago, legal historians have not been able to understand or to interpret the evidence of their own courts.

Not that there has been no concern with the conflicting oral and written legal traditions, for legal history is a library in itself, but that the clearest survival of the oral tradition should be overlooked by the profession that keeps it alive is what makes Brownson's comment so *a propos*. How much Brownson knew of law is immaterial, for his remarks are not useful for their historical validity. In fact, it is probably because he knew so little of law that he could make these broad generalizations, taking his starting point from Daniel Webster's use of common law in the Dartmouth Case, his views follow:

"The distinguishing excellence of the common-law system is, that it is *lex non scripta*, unwritten law, that is, a living tradition, in the reason, the conscience, the sentiments, the habits, the manners, and the customs of the people, and therefore in some sense independent of mere political organizations, and capable of surviving even their most violent changes, and of preserving a degree of order and justice among individuals, when the political authority is for the moment suspended or subverted. It is probably owing chiefly to the fact that the common law is an unwritten law, a living tradition preserved by the people themselves, and administered by an independent judiciary, that political revolutions in England and in this country preserve a character of sobriety and reserve in comparison with those of the continent of Europe. The continental nations have inherited the civil law, the old Roman law, which is a system of written law and theoretically in the keeping of the prince, beginning and ending with the political sovereign. Under this system of law the sovereign is the fountain of justice, as he must be under every system of mere written law; the people are trained for the sovereign, and have no established law to guide or regulate their conduct where he fails to express in a formal manner his will. The state everywhere takes the initiative, and the people without it are incapable of any orderly or regulated civil activity. Hence, whenever the political power receives a shock, all law is suspended, and the judiciary can perform legitimately none of its functions. Consequently, political revolutions in the continental nations throw the whole of society into disorder, and subvert all social as well as political relations. The people receiving the law immediately from the sovereign, or written codes promulgated by the sovereign and not having it in their own life, living in their own traditions, in their own habits, manners, and customs, are without law, and destitute of those habits of thought and action which would restrain them within moderate limits, and consequently are left liable to run into every imaginable excess.

"But the common law, being an unwritten law, and living in the habits and manners of the people, gives them a sort of self-subsistency independent in a degree of mere political power, and operates to restrain and regulate their social conduct, even when that power is temporarily overthrown or suspended. As long as the people remain in any sense a living people, the law survives, and survives as law, and preserves among them, in the midst of the most violent political convulsions, the elements of liberty and social order. England has gone through many changes, religious and political, but we have never seen English society wholly dissolved, or the main current of private and domestic life wholly interrupted, or even turned far aside from its ordinary channel. She has survived all her changes, and amid them all she has preserved her private and domestic life, social as distinguished from political order, but slightly impaired. She preserved a certain degree of individual freedom, to some extent the rights of persons and things, even under the Tudors, and something of 'social order under the commonwealth, which she has continued to do even under the modern Whig rule and a reformed parliament. Much the same may be said of this country during what we call our revolution. There was a time when our political constitutions were suspended, when the political authority was, as we may say, in abeyance, latent, undeveloped, potential, not actual; yet we did not fall into complete social disorder. Irregularity there certainly was, but the courts and the common law remained, and justice still continued to be administered, in the way and in the sense with which our people were familiar, and to which from time immemorial they had been accustomed. In France and other continental countries, the case has usually been different. The subversion of political power there subverts society itself, save so far as it may be preserved by religious institutions, and the people seem destitute of all recuperative energy, or power in themselves to re-establish order; and if they do it at all, it is either through a military chieftain, or by a restoration. These different results, we think, are owing, not to difference of race or blood, or to different degrees of intelligence or moral virtue, as some in our time pretend, but mainly, if not solely, to the difference there is between a system of written and a system of unwritten law.

"The great disadvantage of the European continental nations is in the fact that they have no common law, and no civil law, but written law. These nations are the heirs of the Roman empire, and their civil law is substantially the old Roman law, and like all law embodied in codes is inflexible, and depends for its operation entirely on the political sovereign, who is supposed to prescribe and to administer it, either in person or by his ministers. It has no power to adapt itself to unforeseen emergencies, and to operate regularly in the midst of disorder. Between the written civil law and the unwritten common law, or between the Roman and the English systems, there is a fundamental difference. The Roman law extends only to cases foreseen and provided for, the common law to all cases not taken out of its jurisdiction; the former is of gentile origin, simply modified by the Christian emperors so as not to exclude Christian faith and worship; the latter is of Christian origin, and grew up among the Anglo-Saxons as they were converted from paganism and entered under the guidance of the church upon the career of Christian civilization. The common law starts from the principle that society and the state are for man, and it seeks primarily the protection of private rights, the rights of persons and of things; the Roman starts from the heathen principle that man is for society, and society for the state, and it seeks primarily the protection of public rights, or the rights of the prince. The former abhors despotism, the latter abhors anarchy, the one makes the state absolute, supreme, omnipresent, the other presupposes a power above the state, limits the political power of the state, and asserts a law to which the state itself owes obedience, which subsists, and can, when need is, operate without the express sanction of the political sovereign. The Roman law knows no people but the state, the common law recognizes the people, so to speak, as a power distinct from, and capable of surviving, the state. A nation that has been trained under the common-law system may become an orderly republic; a nation trained under the Roman-law system can never be other than monarchial in effect, whatever it may be in name and pretension or at the furthest a close aristocracy. These are some of the characteristic differences between the two systems, and they sufficiently explain the different results of English or American revolutions from those of continental Europe.

"The essential difference between the two systems does not consist in the mere difference between their respective special provisions, which could easily be made the same in both, but in their general principles, the one as the written law of the prince, and the other as the living traditional law of the people, originating and living in their very life as a people. That the advantages are all on the side of the latter, or the English system, we think must be obvious to every lawyer and every well-informed statesman. It is therefore with pain that we find our politicians ascribing what is excellent in our institutions, what constitutes the chief protection of liberty and order among us, to our mere political organization, and overlooking the merits of the common law, the immense superiority of an unwritten over a written law, and seeking to abolish it, and to substitute a written code in its place. The common law, as an essentially unwritten law, living in the traditional life of a people, can never be introduced into a nation whose character is already formed. It must be born and grow up with a nation. Consequently, when once eliminated from the life of a people, it can never be replaced. Once gone, it is gone forever. It was born with the birth of England as a Christian nation, and grew up with it as the civil part of its Christian life. It became the public reason, the English commonsense, and to it we must attribute the marked superiority of England and her institutions in the middle ages, and even in modern times, over the continent of Europe. Happily England, in casting off, in the sixteenth century, the religion which gave her the common law, did not cast off the common law itself. She preserved it; slightly marred, no doubt, in its beauty and symmetry, yet she preserved it in its substance; and from her we have inherited it, and it should be our study, as we detest anarchy and love liberty, to transmit it unimpaired, in its purity and integrity, to our latest posterity. A richer legacy, aside from the Christianity which gave it birth, we could not even wish to bequeath to future generations."

H. A. Innis in *Changing Concepts of Time* discusses Roman and Common Law traditions. Besides Brownson he appears to be the only writer who has been aware of the conflicting social and intellectual currents stemming from these traditions.

Carroll C. Hollis

THE BREAKTHROUGH FROM LINEALITY
IN MILITARY OPERATION ORDERS*

INTENTION, SITUATION, APPRECIATION:

The purpose of the operation order is to communicate the intention of the commander to subordinates responsible for its execution. In warfare the aim of the commander is to destroy the will of the enemy to resist. The particular means selected by him to achieve this end constitutes his INTENTION.

In order to carry out his intention effectively, the commander must take into account all factors in the SITUATION, such as the disposition of the enemy's forces, his own forces and those of his allies. The nature of the terrain, etc. He must engage in an orderly process of reasoning, leading to a plan of operations, known as an APPRECIATION OF THE SITUATION.

The trained soldier habitually thinks in terms of the appreciation; and the appreciation is carried out at all levels of operation, from a Churchill planning global strategy, to the G.I. heaving a hand grenade into an enemy position. The appreciation may thus be an almost instantaneous and instinctive mental process, or it may take a written form, according to the complexity of the matter and the exigencies of the situation. All appreciations follow an accepted logical sequence:—

(a) The aim which is to be attained.
(b) Factors which affect the attainment of the aim.
(c) The courses open to our own side and that of the enemy.
(d) The plan.

*The military terminology and usage referred to in this study is that of British and Commonwealth armies. The views expressed are those of the author, and should not be taken as necessarily reflecting official opinion.

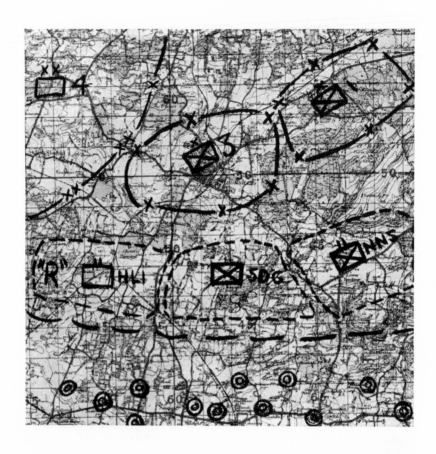

The reproduction above represents the static map with the dynamic, shifting, ideogramic language of the talc overlay. Each symbol has its meaning, from the basic symbol for a unit or formation to the symbol representing an infantry company of the Stormont, Dundas and Glengarry Highlanders.

To summarize this brief excursion into military terminology: the term "appreciation of the situation" means nothing more than the orderly sequence of reasoning leading logically to the best solution of a problem. In the field the plan, or *intention* of the commander is communicated to the subordinate officers responsible for its execution in the form of an Operation Order, or O O.

The O O:

The essence of the operation order was expressed concisely by the Centurion who said, "For I am a man having authority who saith unto his servant, do this, and it is done." Obedience, rightly understood, is a matter not only of the will but of the intellect. To be properly obeyed an order must be perfectly clear, whether given verbally or in writing. Hence the *form* of an operation order is of the greatest importance. The tragic futility of the glorious Charge of the Light Brigade at Balaclava may be attributed to defect in the form of operation order in use at that time. This defect was in itself rooted in the then prevailing traditional military concept, "theirs not to reason why".

The form of written O O used by our army today has been developed through a process of trial and error, with the object of communicating the intention of the commander fully and completely. If an order fails to do this due to inaccuracy, ambiguity or imprecision of language, the consequences may be disaster or defeat. The loss of a kingdom may thus be due to the lack of a horseshoe nail—or to a slip-shod word in an operation order. For these reasons the written O O follows a rigid form, and employs a special military language.

The sequence of an O O closely corresponds to the appreciation of the situation upon which it is based. It takes the form of five paragraphs, as follows:—

1. SITUATION
2. INTENTION (Now termed MISSION in conformity with U.S.A. practice)
3. EXECUTION
4. ADMINISTRATION AND LOGISTICS
5. COMMAND AND SIGNALS

One aspect of this form of order is of special significance today. This is the extent to which the subordinate is enabled to participate in the commander's reasoning process, and thus apply his intention to a swiftly changing situation. This aspect will be explored in some detail later.

The Language of Military Symbols:

The needs of the written operation order have required the creation of a special language of communication, which the staff officer in the field must master. The purpose of this language is twofold: to assure precision and completeness of statement; and through concision to speed up the process of communication. There are three closely related elements in this language; namely, the use of an official military terminology, the reduction of terms in common use to authorized abbreviations, and the development of an elaborate code of conventional military symbols of a visual or *ideographic* character.

The first of these elements calls for little comment, for the employment of an exact terminology is characteristic of all specialized professional fields today. Army terminology is, however, uniform, and defined by high authority in accordance with official doctrine.

Military abbreviations are also standardized. There are about 600 authorized general abbreviations used in the field, in addition to abbreviations for the designations of individual units and formations. Single words may be abbreviated; for example *arty* for artillery, *asst* for assistant, *aslt* for assault. A large proportion of the abbreviations used are in the familiar form of "alphabet soup", such as APO for Army Post Office, ACBO for Assistant Counter Bombardment Officer, AVGAS for Aviation Gasoline. To enliven the task of memorizing this formidable code, Army Schools of Administration resort to the method of the oldtime spelling bee.

However, of much greater significance and interest than this somewhat obvious form of shorthand, is the extensive use which has come to be made of the conventional symbol, or ideograph, with its potentialities of instantaneous visual communication of ideas. The most outstanding example of the development and employment of a specialized ideographic language for the purposes of warfare is the military map.

The Military Map:

Today the military mind has become completely dependent upon the map, as providing the framework for all thinking or planning of a strategical, tactical or logistical nature. The map provides the means for dealing with the space-time factors inherent in all operations. The military map, at its present stage of evolution, is a depiction of terrain in two-dimensional terms by means of conventional symbols; and it is drawn in accordance with two distinct proportional scales, one for horizontal measure and one for vertical.

The soldier has always depended upon maps, however crude in form, in order to visualize or project the tactical problem. The history of the military map reveals a periodic swing between the two opposing poles of the abstract symbol and pictorial representation. A brief examination of this historical pattern may serve to throw some light on the dilemma faced by the modern map-maker presented with "ocular" devices such as the air photo-lense, the air-borne television camera, and radar.

Primitive age: The map of the barbarian warrior was typically a sketch-map drawn in the sand with sword point, or a casual construction of twigs and pebbles. It was abstract. It had no scale. It was ephemeral.

Classic age: The elaborate maps of the Romans were essentially road-maps. Roads, camps, fortifications and towns were indicated by conventional symbols. Their locations were plotted in accordance with a horizontal scale determined by pacing. The natural terrain of mountain, forest and stream formed a background, shown in pictorial terms and then only if of military concern.

Medieval age: The map became a pictorial fantasy, combining the factual and the fabulous. Scale became subjective, and was wildly distorted by the imagination.

Renaissance age: Military maps were made for and by the professional soldier. The cartographer's aim became accuracy and objectivity. The new arts of navigation were employed, and space became enmeshed in Latitude and Longitude. The crowded maps of the age of discovery used conventional symbols freely for the familiar and the known; pictorial representation for the world of the unknown and undiscovered.

Modern age: The rational mind of the eighteenth and nineteenth centuries transformed the military map into a precise, abstract pattern of terrain. Instrument survey established boundaries for everything. A standardized language of conventional symbols was developed. Height was measured, but the map itself became a completely two-dimensional projection.

The present century has witnessed a remarkable extention of this process. Today, almost every square mile of the earth's surface has been meticulously surveyed and mapped for military purposes. The maps of industrial countries, in particular, are incredibly detailed. They show, not only mountain and river, but every fold in the ground and every rivulet or dry gulley; not only town and road, but every tiny hamlet, every lonely habitation of man, every bypath, and even the wayside shrine. The map has become universal. The whole vast complex of our modern communications systems of roads, railways, airfields, telegraph and telephone lines, radio and television installations, which binds civilization together, is mapped in detail. Military maps covering the entire globe are correlated by means of a grid system, like a gigantic and interminable chess board, with each square numbered and further divided by co-ordinates. This makes it possible for a commander, in carrying out his intention, to drop a charge of high explosive, with pin-point precision, upon your doorstep; or if deemed preferable, upon that of your neighbor.

Development of Military Ideograph:

In the context of the military arts the military map may, perhaps, be conceived as being essentially an abstract, highly stylized and completely objective art form, employing a language of conventional symbols. As such its prime purpose is to enable a commander in warfare to visualize the disposition of contending forces, or to project and communicate his visualization to others, in order to control such forces for his own pre-determined ends. Now the map is of its own nature a static representation, but the forces disposed over the ground of the map are dynamic. Hence, the need for an additional code of conventional symbols, which may be superimposed upon the map, to indicate the ever-changing pattern of the mobile forces thus employed.

The code which has been developed consists of about 200 basic symbols, the elements of which can in many cases be combined to form a relatively complex ideograph. Included in this code are basic formation and unit symbols, tactical symbols, symbols for weapons, fire, fortifications and obstacles, and symbols for vehicles and transport movement In the field these symbols may be marked by an officer directly upon the transparent plastic cover of his own map by means of wax pencil, which can readily be erased; or a headquarters may issue a "trace" or "overlay", or print special situational maps, either as a part of a written Operation Order, or supplementary to it.

The Breakthrough from Lineality:

In this outline description of the Operation Order one can discern a classic instance of lineality. The O O reveals typical characteristics of devoted adherence to analysis, logical sequence, exactitude of terminology, and the written statement of reasons for action. The military map provides the frame of reference for action, in a space-time world of chronological-horizontal extension.

Moreover, a curious and ambiguous figure emerges; the Soldier-Scribe, with the pen as ready to his hand as the sword, if not more so. Now, if one may hazard a personal opinion, the Soldier is by nature intrinsically oral in constitution, rather than lineal. The notion of the fighting-man is more than a tradition; it is an archetype. And as archetype it carries such a charge of vitality as to be unfailingly productive of a holocaust of heroes in every generation. Today, the manage-

40

ment of the sacrifice of the young men in their generation is in the hands of the Scribe, himself an archetype of the young man grown old. Ink and not blood now runs in his veins.

This consideration leads us (in terms of lineality) to the concrete reality of the present moment, and raises a practical question of some import. Just how effective is the written Operation Order under conditions of modern warfare? This matter can barely be touched upon here.

The cardinal virtues of the soldier are Courage, Fortitude, Loyalty and Obedience. These moral qualities are unchanged in their essence by the passage of time; but new demands are imposed upon them by the forms of warfare developed in this technological age. Thus, obedience can no longer be blind. Modern war requires the soldier to dedicate not only his will but his intellect; but not to surrender them. Intelligent soldiers are necessary to control, operate and maintain the complicated engines of modern warfare.

In warfare the stage of battle has always been marked by confusion, uncertainty and the unpredictable. Under the conditions of modern warfare, with its accelerated tempo and high mobility in three dimensions, changes in the situation tend to happen with great frequency and bewildering rapidity. Once the commander has committed his forces to battle the initiative passes from him to the subordinate officers in the field who are responsible for executing his orders. But the primitive simplicity of blind obedience to orders no longer fits the conditions of battle. Today the onus lies upon the subordinate to carry out the orders of the commander faithfully to the letter, so long as the situation makes this possible; but if the situation has so changed in the fog of war and smoke of battle that the orders are inoperable, then the responsibility falls upon him to exercise his own initiative and independent judgement in carrying out the intention of the commander, by taking action appropriate to the changed situation.

To formulate such a principle is easy enough; the difficulty is to carry it out in practice. For it imposes an enormous burden upon the subordinate, which may become insupportable; and it generates tensions in the psyche which may prove unendurable. In our own armies this is actually mitigated to a considerable degree by the very rigidity in the form and structure of the written operation order used in the field. For, based as it is upon a known pattern of appreciation of the situation, the subordinate can read back into it much of the process of reasoning followed by his commander in determining his plan. By means of this participation he is enabled to interpret the intention of the commander beyond the strict letter of the written word, and thus effectively adapt his actions to meet the changed factors in the situation.

The ability to execute orders in this flexible manner calls for a special kind of conditioning and training. It appears that a supply of officers possessing this capacity can be assured only in certain Western countries which have evolved forms of political and social life giving scope to the freedom of the individual person. To produce such officers in sufficient numbers would seem to be at present beyond the attainment of the totalitarian type of state. These latter-day frontier barbarians have not yet emerged from the stage of thralldom to the written word. The spell of the Scribe still lies upon them. The frame of reference of their minds and hearts is not totality, but the circumscribed, pedantic tyranny of the lineal.

David Hogg

DADA IN THE DRUGSTORE

> "Truth becomes violence, and a
> passion for the end."—*Blanchot*

> "Beauty will be convulsive, or
> will not be."—*Breton*

To the End of Art

That cultural-philosophic attitude once known as nihilism vanished in
the late forties among the Western intelligentsia not long after the full
implications of contemporary political and technological totalitarianism
sank in. This sudden silence of nihilism at the very moment of the
ratification of its worst predictions and hypotheses by social actuality
(though not by social pretensions) is rather strange. But this anomaly
has received little attention, probably because of our uncertainty whether
a mourning or a celebration is indicated. Is either in order, or even
permitted? Is the missing nihilism dead or alive? Did it die naturally,
or meet with some sort of foul play? Was it of "good" or "evil" character;
was it "guilty" (so that we have no cause for alarm) or "innocent" (so
that there may be a wrong to be redressed?). These are some of the
questions which arise once we overcome the natural indisposition to
inquire too closely into the removal of disturbing elements from the
scene.

The supposed evil or guilt of nihilism may be that it is an attitude which
if adopted seems to make life unendurable by robbing us of all belief
in the benignity of the cosmos and therefore also of all personal security.

43

The individual is thus forced to be constantly on guard, i.e. in a state of continuous muscular-nervous tension (with varying degrees of awareness of this condition, up to the existentialist intensity) and consequently in the absence of faith cannot initiate or perhaps sustain the spontaneous organismic emotions or actions which are the sensations accompanying the state known as happiness or freedom.* Therefore, to the average person, dependent for faith upon the contemporary structure of belief, the nihilist rejection of this structure seems self-evidently perverse and wicked. There are two other types of reactions. One is that of the creative person who is himself alienated from contemporary beliefs and values; he can agree to their negation, but only with the concomitant affirmation of a new set of values which he believes it possible to create. Thus to him the situation of total or near-total disbelief created by the nihilist is only a *hypothetical* or possible attitude—possible if he himself should lose faith in regenerative or recreative power. The third type of reaction may be described as pseudo-creative (for this reason it has confused or entrapped many genuinely creative people in the past—and still does). It also arises from the twentieth century's loss of faith in the entire structure of society, but mislocates the source of this malaise ("blood poisoning," "capitalist encirclement") in the guilt or evil of some particular section of the population, which it then proceeds to exterminate. Just because this delusional procedure brings no relief, but rather worsens the situation, it is necessary simultaneously to forcibly repress any further manifestation of nihilism (which would otherwise, in the absence of any genuine faith, truthfully continue). Thus the totalitarian movements, which often enough in the initial phase won the support of genuine artists and others in a state of nihilist disgust with the status quo, on coming to power were forced to turn against these supporters (and vice-versa) or admit failure. It should now be seen that totalitarianism is not nihilist, but *post-nihilist*: it *represses disbelief* in favor of one or another vast system of delusional "beliefs" to which it compels assent.† The very violence and extent of totalitarian efforts to assert and compel belief are the measure of its actual absence among the rulers (ironically enough, the people they torment may be actually innocent of this disbelief).

The position of the nihilist is thus only in a limited, psychologically unsophisticated sense the ultimate in negation and even there as we shall

*Note that "freedom" is thus *biopsychic* and is not and cannot be the attribute of any idea or institution; the confusion of the latter with the former is the basic one of our time.
†In recent editorials *Life* has complained that there were so few writers willing to subscribe to the American version of industrialist megalomania, and try to engender the proper enthusiasm for its hero in the gray flannel suit. Philosophically a long way ahead of this position, but sharing the same premises, are the Communist critics, who do not need to deal with open dissent, but suspiciously charge their writers with failing to put their heart's blood into the engineer in blue serge. In both cases the idealized activity has nothing to do with freedom (on the contrary) so that its triumph cannot produce enthusiasm, and its defeat cannot produce tragedy.

see it has an ambiguous function. For if the essence of totalitarian motivation is to repress and obliterate any expression or even consciousness of an apparently insoluble and intolerable situation (both social and intrapsychic) in favor of some abstract delusional solution; that of the nihilist, in opposition to this, is the recall and expression of the dreadful reality. He thus occupies a position both historically and ontogenetically *intermediate* between the totalitarian and the bourgeois consciousness. From this point of view it was not nihilism itself but precisely its destruction as an intellectual force that signified the final dissolution of European bourgeois society and the beginning of the reactive totalitarian phase. This will become clear only when we try to get deeper into the soul of the nihilist phenomenon. This will also give us the opportunity to deny that Dostoyevsky wrote in vain, and to assert that nothing is needed more at present than his lost art.

It was perhaps he alone who understood that the provocative attitude of the nihilist arose from a last hope. In total despair provocation, or anything else, is pointless because it can lead to nothing: thereafter the human organism (short of death or madness) desensitizes itself and the despair ceases to be felt. The perpetual crises of Dostoyevsky's great novels consist of the torment of faith by disbelief on both the cosmic and interpersonal levels; hence the alternation of wild hope and bottomless despair. The man of true faith (e.g. Alyosha or Myshin) is opposed by the nihilist (the bourgeois, historically their predecessor, plays only a minor part in the drama) and struggles to save his soul, or power of belief. The nihilist's ambivalence of love and hatred is due to the temptation of faith (always the most ardent human wish) and on the other hand a fear of a recurrence of that betrayal by the powers that be which made him a nihilist in the first place.

In the famous dialogue between Alyosha and Ivan the crux of the whole matter (of the whole of Dostoyevsky's work, in fact) is whether it is possible to retain (for Ivan, to regain) faith despite the evil and injustice of the world, particularly to children who more obviously have done nothing to deserve it. Alyosha manages this belief, in part because of a relative lack of exposure to evil, and in part because of the strength of a faith which, we observe empirically and learn theoretically from psychoanalysis, comes from a favorable, relatively trauma-free childhood making possible a continued mood of what Erik Erikson for example calls "basic trust".* Ivan does not have it. He cannot accept injustice and go on believing. Here there is the tragic contrast between two modes of integrity; the integrity of faith as against the integrity of the will. This

---

* "Childhood and Society." For this aspect, see also M. F. Ashley Montagu, "The Direction of Human Development."

latter is not exactly pride: it is the natural scope of the totally organized consciousness which is unable to exclude the fundamental questions from concern, the way the average person, like Dmitri, can do so, for the length of time it takes to live and die; or cannot, like Alyosha, believe that there is some force or principle in the cosmos that does or will forbid evil and suffering beyond a certain point. But this perception of cosmic indifference or injustice is what separates Ivan from Alyosha, as Job from his friends, and since Alyosha can do nothing about it, cannot remove that injustice (which would restore Ivan's faith) he cannot save Ivan, who eventually kills himself. "If there is no God, anything is possible:" i.e. there is no security or sanctuary for the human soul.

The rejection of faith by the nihilist is in a sense only the recognition that it has ceased to exist: his exposure of the sham has also the implied demand for the restoration of the real thing. Ivan, however, was a primitive type of nihilist, ontogentically still close to the creator type— later nihilists were unable to express that implied demand at all, because the extremity of suffering sooner or later inhibits the power of expression, and were even to deny it. (This shades off into the psychopathic personality type). However, the problem with the creative type is the *restoration* of true faith and not (as with both bourgeois and totalitarian) the *repression* of the nihilist vision. To the creator, the latter reaction does not signify an improvement, but a worsening in the psychological situation. For he sees that what is primarily involved is a repression of the *demand* for real faith which the nihilist is inversely expressing: in repression there has been a *further* loss of faith, that in the possibility that this demand could be met.* The creator is thus placed in an unenviable isolation from the existing cultural situation, for his perception of the falsity of both bourgeois and totalitarian pseudo-affirmations seems to put him on the side of mere defeatism, all the more so when no conceivably possible new solution has emerged as yet. Like "The Idiot" he is stuck with the belief in something which does not exist in actuality, but only as a possibility.

In nineteenth-century Europe, art became self-conscious of its anomalous situation within the growing rigor mortis of world rationalism, and developed a sort of ghetto psychology. Lautréamont and de Sade were isolated predecessors; the real beginning of this tendency was probably with Baudelaire and his discovery of Poe—that is to say of the intrapsychic horrors which civilization had repressed. The premonitions of these original avantgardists seemed a little artificial and unreal, though shocking; they now seem equally unreal, but not shocking, because in that effect they have been surpassed by contemporary events, which have also preempted reality.

---

*Cf. the existentialist para-Stalinist development.

46

The literary-artistic avantgarde career of the nineteenth century was made possible by the artist's knowledge of his isolation from society. (This was also the "class-conscious" isolation of the creative faculty within world rationalism.) The pressure upon the artist was tremendous, as was also on the other hand his new freedom from old restrictions (perhaps an illustration of Toynbee's concept of "challenge and response"). It is not necessary here to recount the triumphant polycourse of art in this period; it is probable that without this unique situation it would never have been initiated; and certain that this retirement within the ghetto of the function itself was the self-preservation of art and that without this there would not have been art as both a solace and a reminder that a deeper existence underlay the rationalist pseudo-affirmations. Yet this separation of the avantgarde from society was not *in itself* a desirable or even in the end a viable thing. If the social situation were to remain more or less stable or permanent it is true that the ghetto-situation might have gone on existing indefinitely (as with the medieval Jews). But world rationalism was not a stable situation, on the contrary a highly dynamic one, whose nature dictated (through science, industrialization, social control) increasing pressure and impositions upon the biopsychic integrity of the individuals composing it (with particular attention to the naïve, the emotional, the creative) in short, upon the former mode of life which it was replacing. Impressionism, for example, was doomed along with its psychogenesis: this dazzling vision of the beauty of all the girls and foliage left in the nooks and crannies of industrialization could not survive the entry of the leaders of human consciousness into the totalitarian phase: even though thereafter women, trees, fields still existed, they had lost their conviction. The desperate, collaborationist, anti-Impressionist *acceptance* of the destructive power ("When a libidinal goal idea is suppressed, the instrument of suppression becomes the bearer of the libido"—Stekel), meant that where art, though aware of its isolation within society, had believed it had a place and function in this very respect, it had been driven to doubt this too. The cubist and especially futurist pictures offer a blackboard demonstration of the invasion of the artist by mechanical rigidity: on the other hand, the artistic function temporarily and relevantly continued.

But the general catastrophe of 1916—the first irrefutable demonstration of the ominous realities underlying "progress" discredited even this equivocal attitude to the scientific-industrial occupation forces. Russian nihilism had never looked upon art as a sanctuary and therefore (as with Dostoyevsky) was early forced to a totalitarian crisis. But that unique contribution of the French to cultural history (later exported to other countries, reaching America in the twentieth century, and even now retaining certain universal prestige) was just this conception of art as a priceless function which must, could, and should exist in isolation from and often in opposition to the rest of society. We have just perceived that this innovation, brilliant though it was, could not last forever, just because its avantgarde vitality would force it toward the attempt at a new solution for a problem growing increasingly worse. But since art seemed powerless to affect this totalistic crisis it itself began to seem pointless in anything but the academic sense—i.e. as a function dependent upon and subservient to a non-creative and anti-organic society. Though this sense (then as now) became the prevalent one, the genuine artist could not accept it. And he could not reject it either without an ominous consequence which only the Dadaists were willing to face. This was a final turning against the French tradition of an eternal but fruitful separation of art from anti-creative rationalist society, in favor of a position now becoming identical with Russian totalistic nihilism.° So the rejection of the false and the struggle for the creative had led to a loss of faith not only in Western civilization but also in all those elements actually or apparently striving toward amelioration or revolution, and this corrosive doubt, especially as all living religions had collapsed, was bound in the end to reach the supposed inviolable sanctuary of art. This sanctuary was also that of the human soul, and there was then no other.

On this event the Dada Kirilov, Jacques Vaché, was to conclude, with a scornful smile: "L'art est une sotisse." Stupid that is, in naïvely supposing that the sanctuary could continue to exist, to give solace and hope, indefinitely regardless of events going on without. A certain cosmic inexperience of the French had once made this believable; but it would never again be possible to be stupid in this way: civilization was approaching its totalitarian pedagogues.

It seemed no longer possible to make any sense out of life, and it was the horror of this situation that the Dada movement tried to communicate. This was the situation which gave their chaotic "art" its peculiar quality: it was not really art since art cannot arise in the absence of some irreducible quantity of faith; but on the other hand it was paradoxically closer to the true situation than that work which did manage to get created regardless of its abstract value. It had in this respect, like Impressionism, become academic.

Here the more profound attachment to art consisted in precisely the power to negate it when its application had become meaningless. Here is something to marvel at, here is something for the Master of Irony!

°Tristan Tzara, in a Dada manifesto of this period: "No more painters, no more writers, no more musicians, no more sculptors, no more religions, no more republicans, no more royalists, no more imperialists, no more socialists, no more bolsheviks . . . enough of all these imbecilities, no more anything, *nothing, nothing, nothing.*"

But the Dadaists accepted this necessity without evasion, knowing that to do so meant the destruction of their own artistic power, for only garbage and not art can be created in the absence of a faith which they were forced to relinquish in order to stay in contact with the actuality— it was as if Theseus had seen Adriane's thread come to an end before the Minotaur was sighted. And yet they went on, out of the only hope remaining to them, of the *efficacy* of their own disaster; which efficacy, no doubt, in turn might have yet saved them.

The deliberate reduction of all form or value to the meaningless was the guiding principle of Dada: applied, there resulted what might be called *ars interruptus*. The reading of a play by Shakespeare, for instance, would be drowned out by the ringing of bells; a periodical would be published with blank pages only; a toilet bowl would be solemnly entered in an exhibition of sculpture. In painting, plastic forms would be destroyed by the introduction of mechanical images or even objects: chaotic colleges sometimes involved printed words—the functional anti- thesis of visual experience—and this became a modernist cliché. "Poems" were written which were mere lists of objects or even of the letters of the alphabet (this latter production by Aragon expressed the complete paralysis of creation before pedagogy). All these meant the imposition of the will of an anti-organic environment upon the human soul by a cruel and watchful interruption of all the beginnings of sincere expression.

Here there should be denoted the different types of response to Dada. It was no doubt mainly the devotees of the more conventional, now academic types of art who rioted at the Dada exhibitions: these found unbearable and unbelievable the reduction of art to the meaningless. These less sophisticated people had not yet recognized or accepted the direction in which Western civilization was moving. This main body was only to catch up with the avantgarde in this degree of sophistication (or loss of faith) some years later, in the totalitarian movements. Initially, however, this violent rejection, rioting and police intervention served to protect the bourgeois ego, but at the cost of awareness of a social disease—and for this temporary anethesia millions were later to pay in wars, purges, and gas chambers. The totalitarian ideocrat, unlike the artist, was to refuse to admit his own despair (because of his purely mechanical ego-strength knowing no other value but its own survival) and was to project it on to various delusional enemies, to destroy it there.

The second type of reaction was that of those nihilists who *enjoyed* the spectacle of the crushing of art, of the hope of the creative spirit, and often enough encouraged or even financed those artists who could give them this pleasure—a reaction which the artists themselves noted with more or less disquietude. For it was not this sinister *acceptance* of his

49

work that the Dadaist really desired, but the opposite, its *rejection*: he had secretly hoped to provoke the revulsion of some vital counterforce to evil and falsity which he had assumed must still exist somewhere in men, society, the Gods, or the cosmos, and thereby force the restoration of the faith. Blasphemy is always an appeal for this restoration, and as such means that some hope remains. The really complete despair cannot express or finally even feel itself at all. The artists could not believe that there did not exist somewhere people or forces which would respond to Dada provocation with effective countermeasures. But the imagined benign and potent counterforce did not exist. In Hannah Arendt's fine phrase, in *Origins of Totalitarianism*, p. 327, "the avantgarde did not know that they were running their heads not against walls but against open doors." They saw that there was to be no creative response to their appeal, that their hypothesis of total negation was indeed the truth. So the expression of this meaninglessness became horrid too. The laughter and cynical applause of these Paris and Berlin art-patrons began to affect the Dada artist just as that of the crowd below strikes the ears of the prospective suicide as he pauses at the edge of the roof. George Grosz has related in *A Little Yes and a Big No*, p. 157 ff., how, no longer able to bear this sort of "success" he fled the deadly nihilism of Berlin for the obscure and relatively untroubled suburb of Bayside, L.I.

Some prominent Dadaists went insane; others committed suicide—the inimitable Jacques Vaché was to do so and take an unwary friend along with him as a final Dada joke. Others diverted the shock into the turbines of abstract surrealist theories. Many of the latter were eventually and logically to land in the Communist Party. All of these reactions had substantially the same meaning: the beginning of the post-nihilist era which has as its basis the masking of individual biopsychic despair by abstract social delusions.

In our century the very existence of art for this reason has been called in question by the vast totalitarian powers created in every area of life by rationalist megalomania. Long before this process found its political expression, it was perceived by the Dadaists, and their particular mode of reaction, however worthless it may appear to formalist aesthetic criteria, is as painfully relevant now as it was then. Those concerned with social affairs must learn sometime that there is no substitute for the prescience of the artist. Where that is absent rational calculation has proven worse than useless.

In this bitter Thermopylae of art, the Dadaist warning that art itself could no longer be taken for granted, might have been couched as a paraphrase of Nietzsche: "Could it be possible! This old fool in the academy hath not yet heard of it, that *Art is dead!*" This is what

Duchamp was saying when he painted a moustache on the Mona Lisa (among things of mythological° and psychoanalytic† interest) and those who decry this act don't know what integrity is. A sort of integrity, moreover, to be followed by the consequences of its crushing defeat: lifetimes of creative silence, so that there would be nothing to show for this inflexible loyalty but apparent total ruin. "Behold, he putteth no trust in his servants, and his angels he hath charged with folly."

> "Gentlemen, I am joking, and I know myself my jokes are not brilliant, but you know you can't take everything as a joke. I am, perhaps, joking against the grain. Gentlemen, I am tormented by questions, answer them for me."—*Feodor Dostoyevsky.*

The Return of the Repressed

Did Dostoyevsky libel the Russian social rationalists and reformists, the liberals and socialists, by intentionally or otherwise confounding them with criminals and nihilists? Certainly this has been a theme of Dostoyevsky criticism from that time to the present day. Or was this "confusion" in some way the insight of genius?—a possibility suggested to the world by, among other Communist phenomena, the Moscow Trials of the thirties, and which since then has been hovering in the background in the manner of Hamlet's Ghost. Though difficult to reject, it has been even more difficult to accept—critical attention shifted hastily to Henry James and still later to nothing at all. There has been no serious attempt to learn from Dostoyevsky in more than a decade. (It is interesting to hear that a limited "rehabilitation" of Dostoyevsky has recently taken place in Russia, simultaneously with the exposure of Stalin.)

The problem is in what way the vision of Dostoyevsky is true. The liberals and socialists, now as then, indignantly denied that they were actually criminals and nihilists—on the contrary! they retorted, it is *we* who wish to bring about a rational order. How do we reconcile this defense with our feeling of Dostoyevsky's terrible persuasiveness?

We can do so, I believe, once we grasp the layer-construction of the human biopsyche, and the peculiar ability of the rational and abstract level to superimpose itself upon and replace modes of *feeling.* Thus Dostoyevsky's accusation of nihilism, like Kierkegaard's accusation of the absence of real faith, was directed not toward that which was evident and expressed on the rational surface layer, but toward the

°Cf. Robert Graves' "White Goddess".
†Cf. Montagu, op. cit.

51

deeper and hidden emotional condition. This, however, is just what the rationalists had succeeded in *repressing*, and therefore in relatively good conscience could deny their nihilism. *They did not understand, however, as Dostoyevsky did, that this repression of nihilism left it only more deeply rooted, and historically and characterologically, did not mean the restoration of faith—repressed nihilism is not faith—but a further step away from it.*

The vast and compulsive repression of this nihilism in favor of abstract pseudo-affirmations (while it, of course, continues to exist subsurface) is the psychological and philosophical essence of the totalitarian phenomena and of the post-nihilist era in which we live. In the Anglo-Saxon world for the past decade the neo-bourgeois or neo-conservative trend has been strongly against any suggestion that the fundamental order of things is not sound (just because it so obviously isn't): this is sometimes oddly combined with "sociological" insights into its emptiness. This latter is possible in concomitance with the former because the sociology remains purely non-purposive or intellectual. It is not nihilist because there is no longer available nihilism's sense of *concern*, or its belief in the *efficacy* of disbelief. Today this is absent. Contemporary sociological criticism or "dissent" is meaningless, not because its theses are not occasionally valid, but because it doesn't really care. It is only the intellectual "understanding" or sense of rational virtue that is desired, and not freedom, which is quite something else.

The emergence of surrealism and after the Second War, existentialism, have sometimes been wrongly interpreted as nihilist phenomena. Surrealism represents, I think, a reaction from the Dada abyss, an attempt to retain belief in the social effectuality of art, which Dada correctly denied (this accounts for the increasing sectarianism and irrelevance of surrealism). Existentialism perhaps never believed in art (to it as to our own New Critics only a matter for "explication") and is post-nihilist in that its fundamental character (which gradually became more evident through the development in its political attitude) is not negation or protest but a neo-stoic conformance to the present mode of oppression.

Consequently the psychological insights of Dostoyevsky have been practically lost as far as the present situation is concerned; we feel we cannot make use of them. The repressed nihilism of the Soviet leaders (or of certain colonial "nationalists") which Dostoyevsky would have perceived at a single glance, is now except for an occasional crude blunder veiled from the consciousness of the world. The millions of people who applaud those confident tours are aware that this leadership has in fact the authoritative grasp of the human condition and stands between them and the cosmos—just as once Stalin himself (at who knows what personal cost?) stood between the Central Committee and awareness of the cosmic failure of the Russian Revolution. The vast majority of men ask only to be permitted to believe in the benignity of this cosmos. But this the leadership itself has long ceased to believe in and has been forced therefore to make what one might call almost heroic efforts to master its rising anxiety through either internal or external repression. It is the magnitude of the world psychological disaster which inhibits and intimidates reaction: too much of our own mode of life is implicated.

Similarly, the disappearance of anything which could be called an avantgarde in the post-nihilist era is due to the fact that all the cosmic, holistic problems are now tacitly felt to be insoluble and best left alone. There is no longer a body of people devoted to the genesis and dissemination of innovation for the new is an unforeseen configuration which solves a problem of real concern and is therefore exciting.

This frustration of the creative, of the avantgarde function would naturally engender nihilist reactions if these were not repressed. This pacification has been carried out in the last ten or fifteen years by the former avantgarde ideocracy, a process psychologically equivalent to the Stalinist development after the failure of the revolution. In both cases the repression of nihilist sentiments makes it quite impossible for the true situation underlying the pseudo-affirmations to be contacted. The drift is toward increasing resignation and apathy.

But these nihilisms excluded from an ideocracy now too resigned and anti-creative to allow them expression have in recent years found a subterranean route and emerged in that vulgar and despised medium, the comic-book. This "return of the repressed" took place in a fauvist "lampoon" efflorescence (EH!, PANIC, WILD, RIOT, CRAZY, BUGHOUSE, etc.). From this mêlée the publication called MAD was to emerge victorious both commercially and critically, acknowledged as the most sophisticated and skilful exponent of the new "humor in a jugular vein"—springing no doubt from a now aggravated Bergsonian sense of humor as "something mechanical encrusted upon the living", and continuing where the brilliant Al Capp had begun to fear to tread. Though the medium of the pictorial strip began as humor, as we know, it eventually came to be used also and primarily for all versions of the polytechnic popular culture. MAD is the product of an evolution in the latter which resembles that which we traced previously in "high" culture. The magazine is edited by intelligent men extremely sensitive to the *Zeitgeist*, who happen to be in the comic-book business. "All of us are constantly being bombarded by particles of misplaced schizophrenia," Roger Price says half or possibly three-quarters seriously in his introduction to the first MAD paperback anthology,* "MAD is a Literary Mutation which is caused by the radiations which result from the splitting of personalities."

The split here is between the conventionalities and the underlying emotional actualities which had previously found expression in the Romantic phase of the comic-book medium. These pre-fauvist comic books had managed to give a partial emotional relief in spite of, in co-existence with the split. This is comparable to Romantic or bourgeois art before Baudelaire, springing from the evasion of a direct conflict. For the comic-book artist this meant the overt acceptance of the conventional rules and values and perforce hypocrisy (as G. Legman's *Love and Death* and other books on the subject have pointed out). For example, the ostensible crime-comic theme, "Crime Doesn't Pay" is only a mask for temporary apostasy and enjoyment of "criminal" feelings—and this rationalization tends to wear thin and become difficult to keep up. In fact, MAD emerged at the time of increasing social pressure (or "radiations") upon the comic-books (legal, medical, and police) which was bound to increase the dilemma and sense of interior splitting of the popular artist.

Once this split has been perceived there are two possibilities: the resignation of the artist, the repression of the condemned emotions, or, instead of this return to some form of the prior evasion, a counter-attack upon the repressive values themselves, including those forms of art, which, by accepting or ignoring the limits of rationalist morality, have themselves become repressive.

The creation of MAD was made possible by a rejection of the first course followed by the bulk of the comic books, which appointed a censor and partially inhibited the product. This was the course socially approved and to a degree enacted into law. The other choice was counter-attack. The defiant and mocking self-designation "MAD" meant that these comic-book artists were becoming aware of their isolation: like the "hipsters" they became an "underground" and in thus refusing to relinquish their creative function under pressure acquired integrity.

This dangerous integrity, which led, as we shall see, to a recapitulation of the Dada experience, naturally aroused anxiety and doubt: like that of Dostoyevsky's Underground Man, it had to be protected by self-laceration. The biographical notes of the creators of "The MAD Reader" are characteristic: the editor, chewing gamely on the lemon, says that he "now sees what his ideals, his purpose, his goal should be . . . now understands what is the most precious thing in life . . . mainly, money".

---

*"The MAD Reader." See also two following: "MAD Strikes Back," and "Inside MAD." Some of the more significant material cited below was unfortunately left unanthologized.'

Another of the staff, it seems, "is a complete idiot. He is kept locked in a steel cage and gets paid in raw beef." All this may even be in some sense true (as equivalently for Dostoyevsky's character) but from Plato to Stalin, the virtue of the artist never was, and above all not in our time, the virtue of the tribe. As the Underground Man himself remarks, "He would even risk his cakes and would deliberately desire the most fatal rubbish, the most uneconomical absurdity, simply to introduce into all this positive good sense his fatal fantastic element . . . simply in order to prove to himself—as though that were so necessary—that men are still men and not the keys of a piano."

On the stereotypes of American popular culture and advertising—there has probably never been a more devastating attack than the campaign launched by MAD some time in 1952. Initially MAD concentrated its fire on the Romantic academy, its immediate predecessors, the comic-books conforming to the myths, mores and stereotypes from which belief and vitality had drained. These are inexorably reduced to absurdity by the introduction of reality at appropriate (or inappropriate) moments.

In every possible way, the popular Hero with a Thousand Faces—he who can handle effectively human crises—is thwarted and ridiculed. His Wild West incarnation, the "Lone Stranger" on hearing of trouble brewing somewhere in the distance, leaps for Hiyo Golden in standard operating procedure; however, in the MAD version he misses and lands on his rear. Moodily he trudges back to camp (complete with swimming pool, yacht and portable radio). He starts to get dinner ("This is the life! Out here! Nature! Building a campfire with rustic implements!") The fire, though kindled in approved Boy Scout fashion, fails to ignite. Coming back to earth, the Stranger uses his cigarette lighter. Later he is put through a burlesque stagecoach routine and at the end, fleeing the plaudits of the crowd, once more lands upon harsh reality instead of his horse. The original knight himself, hero of the medieval past, is treated with little more consideration: faced with the crisis, "Prince Violent reacts swiftly and in one smooth motion . . . draws arrow from quiver . . . drops arrow . . . picks up arrow . . . drops bow . . . picks up bow . . . drops quiver . . . picks up quiver, drops helmet and bow . . . picks up bow . . . drops helmet, bow, arrow, chainmail, pants." The contemporary hero of the foreign adventure, "Terry and the Pirates", abruptly tosses his loyal sidekick to the sharks and reveals that he himself is now and always has been a pirate. The hero of the future, "Flesh Garden" (recapitulating the development of monotheism and the subsequent conquest of the natural environment by science), reaches the Promised Planet and overcomes the hawkmen, owlmen, rockmen, treemen, grassmen, only to be captured by the "men-men" and thrown into

55

the sacrifical arena, where he will have to meet some unknown monster. "What kind of creature lies behind that blood-stained oaken door? Could it be worse than the slime-oozing, knife-toothed zork? . . . than the horny, many-clawed zorchton? . . . than the palpitating, limb-ripping zilchtron? . . . Gasp! I can see it now—worse than the zork, more terrible than the zorchton—more horrible than the zilchtron. It's . . . it's . . . MAN!" In this fashion MAD perhaps comes back to the point, after its genocide of the heroes.

Something like the apogee of this encyclopedic irreverence is reached with the unprovoked onslaught on Pogo, who had asked only to live and let live in the swamp—some MAD readers wrote in later to complain that this was really going too far and exceeded "the limits of human decency". At any rate "Gopo Gossum" is introduced with a little philosophic conceit, which might have been drawn from Rousseau: "How why the heck is it the thing to make animals act like men . . . and it ain't never the fashion to make men act like animals—beats us. Anyhow . . ." Gopo returns from a trip to the big city, now—like Comal Nasser—sadly contaminated by Progress. "I been thinking . . . How come our cousins is living in 'spensive pent-houses while we living in a flea-bitten swamp? how come they got automobiles? . . . By ding, let's face it! We ain' big-time." He had conversed with his sophisticated relatives and they had advised him to accept the realities of modern society and abandon the backward mores of the swamp. "We got to fool around with real politics like the Dixon-Yates contrac'!" Sparked by the enlightened Gopo, the political education of the swamp creatures then gets underway at a breakneck pace, despite the warnings of the swamp's Cassandra, the little tadpole: "Oh, please don' go messin' roun' with politics! Don't go looking for trouble! Please, everybody!" Gopo replies as sternly as any other nouveau-Marxiste, "Don't have to go looking! It right here in the swamp!" True enough, while "Li'l Grim-doom's" formerly enigmatic, Zen-like interjections ("XZTW"), with the proper education and environment begin to arrange themselves into the all too recognizable, laconic insignia of big-bureaucratic rationalism: ("TWA, NLRB, CIOPAC, FDRJr, SPCA," etc.) all the swamp creatures soon metamorphose into contemporary political figures, McCarthy, Nehru, Chou-en-lai etc. And the dialogue, now concerned with "the real 100% McCoy politics", grows manic: ("Hoop! Hoop! We is busted into a mess o' parties!") and the once easily "flimflammed" swamp erupts into frenzied para-colonial political struggles until chaos and the inevitable explosion point is reached. Then we see the atomic mushroom cloud rise high above the swamp: so perishes the Eden-dream of the *New York Post*.

As thus the lamps (however shoddy) go out all over American popular culture, a darker mood begins to intrude into what was ostensibly heretofore only good mad fun. "Bringing Back Father" (MAD #17) is a schizoid little piece whose effect is sometimes uncanny. The action is now carried forward simultaneously upon two levels, that of burlesque and that of a kind of depth-analysis, on facing pages—the first, drawn in the bright, glib, sharp style of the original Jiggs & Maggie strip, is a model MAD satire; but on the other page for the first time the Underground Man appears instead of his work, his pitiless satire. The colors darken, the shapes distort, the grim and angular actuality of the Underground permeates everything. "Plenty things we think are funny . . . if we take a second look . . . these things are very serious!" And on these second pages MAD does take a second look at the deeper aspects of its satire upon a satire. "Get up, you worm," snarls "Maggs" after the usual business of preventing, by force and violence, a visit by "Jiggie" to Dinty Moore's for some authentic food (instead of the ersatz petty-bourgeois product) "Get up, and look at all the happy readers smiling at how I knocked you over with the dishes!" Simultaneously, on the next page, as the Underground Jiggie picks himself up slowly from the floor, he is moved to uncharacteristic, genuine protest: "By golly, Maggs, this isn't a very funny matter! . . . Do they realize sometimes a flying dish can break open the scalp and cause serious bleeding? . . . Let the readers hit themselves in the head and see if that pain is funny! . . . Them stars could indicate a brain concussion or injury to the eyeball!" But the attempted crime and punishment goes through several more acts: finally Jiggie grows desperate: "Nobody getting beatings like me can survive! . . . I've *got* to sneak past Maggs! I've got to escape for real!" In the overground strip, he makes his most ingenious attempt to escape yet, which also fails: this time, after the classical reprisals of Maggs, on the Underground page he arises from the pile of broken crockery to give his wife, daughter, and no-good brother-in-law a brutal drubbing, thus shockingly "solving" the repetition-compulsion and bringing the story of Jiggs to a close. Overground, the beneficial consequences of this act are seen: his family gets into line at a corned-beef-and-cabbage party. There a friend of Jiggie's, pleased and amazed at this transformation, comments with social-worker obtuseness upon "the new psychological adjustment to the former vicious marital relationship between you and Maggs". Overground, Jiggie smiles genially; underground he concludes thoughtfully to himself, "It's good to be serious once in a while." Perhaps this mood of discontent stemmed in part from the fact that at this time the whole lampoon-book *Weltanschaaung* seemed to be getting close to MAD's own jugular vein. A horde of cheap imitations had badly hacked up most of the material which MAD might otherwise have ploughed; and had done so, moreover, with so little skill and verve that the act of lampooning or satire itself was coming to seem dull and stereotyped. MAD therefore set out to destroy the stereotype too.

57

("Cut Your Own Throat Dept.") This was already well on the way to the Vachéan apocalypse: though Duchamp had painted a moustache on the Mona Lisa, he did not also caricature himself in the act.* (At this point he disengaged himself entirely from the process and sank into the intricacies of chess.)

The whole bag of lampoon Dada-tricks was "exposed" by the device of simply repeating them as before in a new lampoon story ("Julius Caesar"—MAD #17) but now accompanied with a cold-blooded "explication" by a gray-faced MAD editor. From the sides or bottom of each strip-box, the latter points out, smirking, each mechanism of *ars interruptus*: the insertion into each box of small irrelevant drawings or letterings which break up emotional unity or continuity; the use of the deliberate anachronism; bop or hipster slang "Routine #7, where a person cries so much the tears make a flood!"—(the refusal of and mockery of grief); the similarly-motivated depicture of people perforated by bullets or transfixed by sharp implements, who carry on as before without change or affect; and the random introduction of irrelevant pictures of Marilyn Monroe or, almost equivalently, the atomic bomb. The culmination of "Julius Caesar" is "Routine #13, the trick ending"—it turns out that the protagonists were always in disguise: "Here everyone whips off rubber masks and you find out the hero really isn't the hero . . . the villain really isn't the villain . . . " Then, the other way around? No, for we live in the age of relativity and Hegelian justice (or the Stalin Uncertainty Principle): the protagonists appeal to a still deeper insight, whip off another set of masks, reversing the roles of hero and villain again, then still again, and so forth. This Bolshevik sequence of exposure and counter-exposure is carried out until, with a kind of hysterical repudiation, the caption proclaims: ". . . And I'm not really your MAD writer . . . matter of fact, this isn't really MAD comic-book." The MAD editor in turn unmasks, exposing the face of a pretty girl, and turns a page to show a scene from a Walt Disney innocence-dream. A happy ending, of a sort.

There were thereafter several more issues of the "routine" character which, however, could not stave off the deepening second Dada crisis: the prime characteristic of which is, as we saw, the turning of the artist against art itself. And even this anti-artistic pseudo-creation must sooner or later involve that part of the artist temporarily salvaged by the process, until the point of exhaustion and indifference is reached. "If there is no God, anything is possible."

The "Special Art Issue" (MAD #22) was devoted entirely to the "life

---

*One step from this, Picobia had depicted the modernist idol, Cezanne, as a toy menlsey in a frame. (1920)

and work" of MAD's chief artist, "that miserable two-bit hack . . . From
the moment Bill Elder was born" he started drawing in "chicken-fat"—
(an improbably unintentional euphemism for a certain familiar substance)—thenceforth to be his distinctive medium. MAD traces Elder's
career through his initial "shmears" on various domestic surfaces to more
ambitious projects, which are reproduced with the comment: "Today
his shmears are hung in museums and signed with Elder's various pen-
names such as 'Braque', 'Matisse', 'Picasso', etc." This, however, hardly
indicates the versatility of his genius: "Here is an interesting little ash-tray
he knocked out with his plasticene set, under the pen-name of Benvenuto
Cellini! . . . Another piece of work which he called 'The Thinker'."
Elder then dabbles in abstract art: "his sixth creates a feeling of clashing
harmony, yet an inner tranquillity! In other words [the pain-killing ad-
vertisement is reproduced] Bofferin acts twice as fast as aspirin in this
abstract called 'Urp!' Experimenting roughly along the lines of Marcel
Duchamp's 'Nude Descending a Staircase' young Elder painted this
seventh abstract entitled 'I Dreamed I Descended a Staircase in My
Playtex Underwear'." There is a technical interlude during which Elder
invents photographic realism, the movies, 3-D and Cinemascope, after
which he returns refreshed to "the most brilliant part of his career, when
he did the following paintings: [shown] 'Mona Lisa' (actually Mona
Coznowski); 'Blue Boy'; 'Young Woman With a Water Jug' (here we
see one of Elder's many girl friends, this one just come from the barber
shop, towels and all, was in the act of throwing slops into the back lot
instead of the garbage pail); 'Whistler's Mother' (note the tense expression on the subject due to her son's constant maddening whistling
in the next room which she by the way ended with the small revolver
she has concealed in her kerchief." Finally Elder gets around to the
mystery ceiling of the Sistine Chapel, which it seems was done on the
floor and the whole building then rolled right-side up, like a barrel.

"Bill (Chicken-Fat) Elder now knew how to make all kinds of fine things!
He was now prepared to choose which of these fine things he would
devote the rest of his life to make! And do you know what he chose to
make, dear Reader? . . . Right! . . . He chose to make money!" Further
examples of commercial art are then given the Dada twist (in travel
illustrations airplanes and trains are shown wrecking themselves; pet
hamsters bite the hand that buys them; "Mr. and Mrs. Fred Worceshire-
sauce, popular New York socialites, say 'We keep our swimming pool full
of extra cartons of Herbert Terrytoon cigarettes,'" etc.). Again the
course of unsuccessful nihilism leads to weariness and apathy ("Still
with it, eh? Why don't you do something useful instead of reading this
junk? . . . Anyhow, by this time Elder had worked his way up to the
comic book. This, then, is the golden chapter."). The long repressed

Underground Man makes his second, final and most harrowing appearance on the MAD stage.

"The immortal story of that man out of control, digging through a hole, *Melvin Mole!*" if not precisely immortal, in its own way carries overtones of Kafka, Orwell and Dostoyevsky—and in my opinion is more faithful in spirit and possibly even in aesthetic power to those illustrous predecessors than most of what has been published in recent years as serious fiction.

Melvin Mole is a repulsive baggy-suited little character (file-toothed, rat-nosed, bepimpled) who resembles that caricature of the wild-eyed anarchist, nihilist or degenerate in the pre-totalitarian era, but the subject, as we have seen, has since been lost sight of. This neo-Underground Man, Melvin, is literally underground: his peculiar (perhaps only) talent consists of his ability to burrow with unbelievable cunning underneath all obstacles. The story opens to follow Melvin's trail under a street and into the vault of the "Last National Bank", to the accompaniment of Melvin's obsessional muttering: "Dig! Huh! Dig! Dig! Dig! Dig!" In the bank, however, on the point of collecting, Melvin suddenly notices that the omniscient police have stationed waiting guards there. In febrile but obviously already *anticipated* frustration Melvin discharges a machine-gun in all directions, yelling "John Law! You flatfoots won't put me in jail! Not me! Not Melvin Mole! No, not me! Never!" His subjugation, however, is seen as so inevitable that the artist does not bother to demonstrate it: in the next box we see Melvin being kicked into a cell. While a dozen rifle barrels follow his every move, his custodian (a sort of Porfiry Petrovich) affirms: "You've dug your last hole, Mole! . . . You're under control! Don't try anything! We're wise to your ways! We know about the time you dug your way into Fort Knox [the French Revolution?] . . . We know about the time you dug your way out of Devil's Island [the Russian Revolution?] . . . So don't try anything! *You're heading straight for the electric chair!*" Or historical extinction of the revolutionary spirit? But in leaving Melvin his custodian overlooks a lunch spoon, with which the Mole then proceeds to dig out of jail. Unfortunately when he decides to come up, in mid-city, it is inside a police telephone box (the media of public communications are blocked). (Coppers won't put me in jail! No! Nein! Nicht! Never!") Stripped to his underwear, minus sox, false teeth and excess fingernail, Melvin is tossed back into a reinforced cell. "You slippery litle rat!" his keeper grates, half-admiringly, picking his teeth, "Mole! Yew . . . have . . . dug . . . your . . . last . . . hole! We are putting you in solitary confinement. You won't do it again!" But before leaving, the keeper discards his toothpick and as soon as the door clangs ("Dumb John Law copper!") Melvin is on his way to freedom with it. ("Dig! Dig! Dig! Dig! Dig!") He tunnels a magnificent distance but again comes up prematurely, at a policeman's ball (the media of public entertainment are blocked). Maddened, Melvin blasts away with an automatic, hysterically sobbing: "John Law! Waaah! Haw haw! Haw! Hi hi hi!" Implacably he is re-dungeoned, this time naked and shaved. However, they overlook his nostril hairs (the pitiable remnant of creative power left to totalitarian man) one of which Melvin plucks forth. ("Dig! Dig! Dig! Dig! Dig!") At length Melvin emerges, at the end of his strength: "Puff! Can't go on! Puff! Can't dig another inch! Huh, huh! No jail kin hold Melvin Mole! . . . Huh! Where did I dig to . . . OQP!" He is in the execution chamber; a coffee pot is percolating merrily on the electric chair, and the waiting keeper gloats: "Have a seat, Mole!" So perishes the Last of the Nihilists.°

From the forties, the recent decade of the Age of Anxiety, there has emerged what might be called an "Age of Stupefaction"—that is, of lessening reaction to increasingly powerful crisis-stimuli, and now substantially complete. The impression has solidified that all the cosmic, the fundamental questions no longer exist and perhaps even that they never did. This stolidity and indifference is now the contemporary intellectual mode. Under this surface there lies—historically and characterologically—the repressed anxiety. Under this, the nihilism or disbelief. Under this, the capacity for the expression of grief and anger. Only then does the possibility of real faith or belief arise at all. How to regain this possibility is the fundamental problem of the intellectual (secondarily and to a less intense degree, the general human problem, since it takes its way of living from the leadership). This remains true so far as he deserves to be called an intellectual.†

Unfortunately, the dead hand of the existing social and "intellectual" powers is in opposition to this solution and even to the problem itself. The trend now seems to be to deal with anxiety by drugs. This doubt-engendering emotion can now be practically exterminated (as in Aldous Huxley's incredibly accurate prediction) by the new "tranquillizer" drugs —the use of which is spreading among the ideocracy. This only confirms, however, the philosophic tranquillization carried out in recent years. No doubt it will at length occur to the Communists also that

---

°Having come to the end of this phase, MAD subsequently reorganized as a more conventional "humor" magazine, now including the work of a number of well-known professional humorists. Its own unique and less popular neo-Dadaist flavor has been greatly diluted. The first two issues of the new MAD contained some excellent material, but since then quality has steadily declined. The original editor (Harvey Kurtzman) has since left and his staff have just put out "Trump"—a four-color job which also fails to come up to the old MAD level.
†Paul Goodman drew a similar sketch in vol. 1, no. 1 of *Complex*. Harold Rosenberg, another old avante-garde loyalist, has some cogent remarks on the subject in the December 1956 *Commentary*.

a few carloads of Miltown shipped into Budapest might have saved a lot of trouble.

In this situation, because it is now known that art alone cannot alter the course of events, art cannot be created or responded to in the eager, holistic way it was before: as in late nineteenth-century Europe or the American twenties. There has been little good work, no great innovations, in the past fifteen years. The nature and even the future existence of art is dependent upon some possible future alteration in the *Zeitgeist*. For this the world awaits some new philosophic or psychological concept of reality to set against that of the Marxists. This is itself, however, unlikely to be invented or carried into effect under a state of narcosis. Thus as a potent anti-tranquillizer MAD has probably been of more service to art in recent years than, say, the artistic contributions of Picasso or Hemingway, which in a sense falsify the real picture.*

The standard cover-format of MAD displays a frieze of portraits of the rationalist giants (Socrates, Galileo, Columbus, Copernicus, Pasteur, Freud, etc.)—all fascinatedly absorbed in copies of MAD. Some such reconsideration was attempted here, and may indeed be going on above or below, in the common intrapsychic heaven or hell.

---

*Hemingway's last fisherman vs. elements novel was good in proportion to its distance from the coastline of civilization: when an attempt to *relate* the two was made (the dreadful baseball metaphors) it ruined the novel. Similarly, Picasso conscientiously tries to be a good Communist, but then is forced to blot out the sight of the Communists attacking or suppressing his own work.